W9-CDB-560

Lanford Wilson

Twayne's United States Authors Series

Warren French, Editor

University College of Swansea, Wales

TUSAS 490

LANFORD WILSON
(1937–   )
Photograph by Diane Gorodnitzki

Lanford Wilson

By Gene A. Barnett

Fairleigh Dickinson University

Twayne Publishers
A Division of G. K. Hall & Co. • *Boston*

THE UNIVERSITY OF TOLEDO LIBRARIES

Lanford Wilson

Gene A. Barnett

Copyright © 1987 by G.K. Hall & Co.
All Rights Reserved
Published by Twayne Publishers
A Division of G.K. Hall & Co.
70 Lincoln Street
Boston, Massachusetts 02111

Copyediting supervised by Lewis DeSimone
Book production by Janet Zietowski
Book design by Barbara Anderson

Typeset in 11 pt. Garamond
by Modern Graphics, Inc., Weymouth, Massachusetts

Printed on permanent/durable acid-free paper
and bound in the United States of America

Library of Congress Cataloging-in-Publication Data

Barnett, Gene A. (Gene Austin)
  Lanford Wilson.

  (Twayne's United States authors series ; TUSAS 490)
  Bibliography: p.
  Includes index.
  1. Wilson, Lanford, 1937–   —Criticism and
interpretation. I. Title. II. Series.
PS3573.I458Z59   1987   812'.54   87–5657
ISBN   0–8057–7498–X (alk. paper)

PS
3573
. I458 Z59
1987

For Marj

Contents

About the Author

Gene A. Barnett received the Bachelor of Arts degree from Oklahoma Baptist University, the Master of Arts degree from the University of Oklahoma, and the Doctor of Philosophy degree from the University of Wisconsin, where he wrote a dissertation under the late Professor Harry Hayden Clark. He began his teaching career at Wayne State University in Detroit. Since 1967, he has been a member of the Department of English and Comparative Literature on the Teaneck Campus of Fairleigh Dickinson University. He is the author of several articles, and his Twayne volume on the Irish playwright Denis Johnston was published in 1978. Like Lanford Wilson, he is a native of Southwest Missouri. He lives in Teaneck, New Jersey, but retains strong roots in Wheaton, Missouri, where his family has lived since the 1860s.

Preface

In 1963, Lanford Wilson, then twenty-six years old, handed Joe Cino a copy of a short play called, somewhat poetically, *So Long at the Fair*. Cino was the proprietor, host, guiding spirit, and guardian angel of a coffeehouse theater that was not only "the first . . . developed by the Off Off Broadway movement" but "the only Off Off Broadway organization that was even marginally self-support-ing."[1] Located at 31 Cornelia Street, in the Greenwich Village area of New York City, the Caffe Cino had, by 1963, been in existence for approximately four and one-half years. *So Long at the Fair,* Joe Cino's one-hundredth production, would be Wilson's first. As such, it inaugurated a career that has extended into the mid-1980s and includes thirty-five plays, in addition to a translation of a Russian classic, an opera libretto, and three television plays.

Wilson's career brought the young playwright from Off-Off-Broadway to the Great White Way itself in a mere six years. But the New York premiere in 1969 of *The Gingham Dog* on West 45th Street was inauspicious, for the play closed after five performances and a few previews. The next year brought another major disap-pointment for Wilson in the Off-Broadway failure of *Lemon Sky*. Three years later, however, his great success, the prize-winning *Hot-l Baltimore,* compensated for these earlier disappointments. In 1980, *Talley's Folly* brought its author the Pulitzer Prize for drama and confirmed his reputation nationally.

There have been other peaks in Wilson's career—the triumphant move to Broadway of *Fifth of July* and the vindication of *Lemon Sky* in a late 1985 revival, for example—but most important, there has been a steady flow of both one-act and full-length plays. Other recent revivals and revised versions of earlier plays have attested to the durability of his work. One senses from personal encounters and published interviews that for Wilson, living is synonymous with working at what he terms his "calling." Failure to respond to that "call" is, quite simply, unthinkable—"a sin," as he says. This study ends with a new play on Lanford Wilson's desk—*Burn This*—complete only in the first draft and therefore not considered here.

This book, the first on Lanford Wilson, discusses all his published work and as much as possible of the unpublished work. I particularly wished to give attention, as length allowed, to unpublished material, since it is not easily available. The plays, with only minor exceptions, are considered chronologically. The introductory chapter includes most of the biographical background and a short description of two apprentice works: the very brief *Miss Williams: A Turn* and the previously mentioned *So Long at the Fair.* Thereafter, critical analysis is emphasized over biographical matters. To Wilson's credit, be it said that, unlike a great deal of contemporary theater, his plays withstand close critical scrutiny, even though, as a total body of work, they vary in quality from "unsuccessful" to "great." I find him always interesting and challenging, for his work is that of a committed artist.

The principal aim of this book, then, is to present an overall view of all the playwright's oeuvre and in that presentation to convey some idea of the dramaturgy involved—the themes, characters, structure, and dramatic and literary techniques and devices, showing how they evolve, change, disappear, and reappear as the playwright develops his craft and matures both as an artist and as a man. To conform with the plan for this series, most works are not analyzed in great detail, but taken all together, these discussions will convey, I hope, a total view of the playwright at midcareer.

I thank Lanford Wilson for his time, patience, and assistance as I prepared this book. Most of all, I am grateful to him for writing these plays. His agent, Bridget Aschenberg, of International Creative Management, Inc., has been kind and efficient in answering questions and providing me with both published and unpublished material. I am also deeply grateful to Warren French for his interest and encouragement throughout this project. Three of my colleagues at Fairleigh Dickinson University have given me special assistance: Bernard Dick read some of the manuscript in the early stages and made helpful suggestions, and Doris Auerbach and Vernon Schonert helped me with translations and interpretation. The staff of the Weiner Library on the Teaneck Campus, particularly Judy Katz and Laila Rogers of the Reference Department and Mary McMahon and Judy Barrett of the Periodicals Department, were prompt in securing materials for me and kind and patient in other matters. Melissa Abramovitz and Jo-Anne Whitfield were efficient and expeditious as they assisted me in the preparation of the manuscript. Finally, a special word of thanks to my good friend and colleague, Lois

Gordon, chairman of the Department of English and Comparative Literature, who not only encouraged me but shared her experience, while carefully reading portions of the manuscript in its final stages.

Gene A. Barnett

Fairleigh Dickinson University

Chronology

1937   Born in Lebanon, Missouri, 13 April, to Ralph and Violetta Wilson.

1942   Parents divorced; moves with mother to Springfield, Missouri.

1948   Mother remarries (Walt Lenhard); family moves to a farm near Ozark, Missouri.

1954–1955   Sees *Brigadoon* and *Death of a Salesman* at Southwest Missouri State College and falls in love with theater.

1955   Graduates from Ozark High School in May; enrolls at Southwest Missouri State College, Springfield, for the 1955 summer session and the fall quarter.

1956   Reunion with his father in San Diego; attends San Diego State College while working at an aircraft factory.

1957   Moves to Chicago; works as an artist in an advertising agency.

1959   Switches from writing short stories to plays; enrolls in a play-writing class at a University of Chicago extension.

1962   Arrives in New York City, 5 July; lives in Greenwich Village.

1963   January, sees production of Ionesco's *The Lesson* at the Caffe Cino, which points him toward Off-Off-Broadway as a place where he might have plays performed; gives Joe Cino *So Long at the Fair,* which is produced at the Caffe Cino on 25 August; *The Bottle Harp*

1964   *Home Free* and *No Trespassing,* 16 January, Caffe Cino; *The Madness of Lady Bright,* 19 May, Caffe Cino.

1965   *Balm in Gilead,* 20 January, La Mama Experimental Theater Club; *Ludlow Fair* (written 1963), 1 February, Caffe Cino; *This Is the Rill Speaking,* 20 July, Caffe Cino; *The Sand Castle,* 22 September, La Mama

Experimental Theater Club; *Miss Williams: A Turn* (written 1962), 3 November, a one-performance benefit for La Mama Experimental Theater Club; *Days Ahead* and *Sex Is between Two People,* 28 December, Caffe Cino.

1966   *Wandering,* 10 April, Caffe Cino; *The Rimers of Eldritch,* 13 July, La Mama Experimental Theater Club.

1968   *Untitled Play,* 26 January, Judson Poets' Theater, New York City; *The Gingham Dog* (written 1966), 26 September, Washington Theater Club, Washington, D.C.; *Sa Hurt?*

1969   *The Gingham Dog,* 23 April, Broadway; *Stoop* presented as part of *Foul!,* 28 November, on Channel 13, "New York Television Theater"; Circle Repertory Company organized.

1970   *Lemon Sky* (written 1968), 26 March, Studio Arena Theatre, Buffalo; *Serenading Louie,* 1 April, Washington Theater Club; *Lemon Sky,* 17 May, Off-Broadway.

1971   *Sextet (Yes),* 11 February, Circle Repertory Company; *The Great Nebula in Orion,* 18 February, Stables Theatre Club, Manchester, England; libretto for Lee Hoiby's opera, *Summer and Smoke,* adaptation from Tennessee Williams's play, 19 June, in St. Paul, Minnesota; *Victory on Mrs. Dandywine's Island;* buys 1845 farmhouse in Sag Harbor, Long Island.

1972   *Ikke, Ikke, Nye, Nye, Nye,* 13 January, Yale Cabaret, New Haven, Connecticut; *Summer and Smoke,* 20 March, New York City Opera, Lincoln Center; *The Great Nebula in Orion,* 21 May, Circle Repertory Company; *The Family Continues,* 21 May, Circle Repertory Company.

1973   *The Hot-l Baltimore,* 4 February, Circle Repertory Company; reopens at Circle-in-the-Square on 22 March; receives the New York Drama Critics Circle Award for Best American Play.

1974   *The Migrants,* 23 February, on television's "Playhouse 90."

1975   *The Mound Builders,* 2 February, Circle Repertory Company.

1976   *Serenading Louie,* 5 May, Circle Repertory Company.

1977   *Brontosaurus,* 25 October, Circle Repertory Company.

1978   *Taxi,* 2 February, on television's "Hallmark Hall of Fame"; *Fifth of July,* 27 April, Circle Repertory Company; *Bar Play.*

1979   *Talley's Folly,* 3 May, Circle Repertory Company.

1980   *Talley's Folly* moves to Broadway, 20 February; awarded Pulitzer Prize for drama; *Fifth of July,* 5 November, Broadway.

1981   *Thymus Vulgaris,* 4 June, Lee Strasberg Institute, Los Angeles; *A Tale Told,* 11 June, Circle Repertory Company.

1982   *Thymus Vulgaris,* part of a triple bill, *Confluence,* 10 January, Circle Repertory Company; *Angels Fall* (commissioned), 19 June, New World Festival, Miami, Florida.

1983   *Angels Fall,* 18 January, Broadway.

1984   Translation of Chekhov's *The Three Sisters,* 23 March, Hartford Stage Company, Hartford, Connecticut.

1985   *A Betrothal* (commissioned); *Talley & Son* (*A Tale Told* revised), 22 October, Circle Repertory Company; *Burn This* completed for 1987 production.

1986   *The Mound Builders,* revised, 30 January, Circle Repertory Company. *A Betrothal,* 30 September, Man in the Moon (pub theater), London (premier).

1987   *Burn This,* 22 January, Mark Taper Forum, Los Angeles; 18 February, Circle Repertory Company.

Chapter One
Biography and Early Work

When Lanford Wilson was a teenager attending Ozark High School in the small southwest Missouri town of Ozark, he and a few other students were sometimes taken over to Springfield, about twelve miles away, to see the plays produced on the campus of Southwest Missouri State College. He does not recall details of these youthful expeditions, but he has charmed more than one interviewer with his enthusiastic account of seeing his first "live" theater other than local high school plays in which he himself participated. "I have no idea how I got there or how I got home," he says now of a trip to see *Brigadoon* in 1954. "All I remember is every single moment of the play. I just remember seeing the play and being mesmerized."[1]

"Magic" is a word Wilson uses to describe another production he saw at Southwest Missouri State in 1955: *Death of a Salesman,* directed by Leslie Irene Coger. It was "the most magical thing I'd ever seen in my life," he says; "the clothesline from the old buildings all around the house gradually faded into big, huge beech trees. I nearly collapsed! . . . It was the most extraordinary scenic effect, and of course, I was hooked on theater from that moment." Looking back, he admits that he was trying "in that first dreadful play . . . to recreate some of that magic. I mean," he emphasizes, "that magic was what I was always drawn to."[2]

Several years later, Wilson was living and working in Chicago, all the time continuing to write short stories, which he had written since boyhood. One day as he was about to begin a story, he realized, perhaps because of its similarity to Tennessee Williams's *The Glass Menagerie,* that the story was really a play. "So I started writing it in play form which, for me at that time, was just dialogue. . . . I instantly knew that was what I should have been doing all along, instantly knew that I was a playwright."[3]

Wilson puts into the mouth of one of his characters his own wonder and exhilaration at the discovery of his "calling." In *Angels Fall* (1982), a young professional tennis player describes his "call" as the "magic that happens and you know who you are": "I hit that first ball and I said, 'This is me. This is what I do. What I do is tennis.' And once you know, then there's no way out." This tennis player is really Lanford Wilson speaking in the native accents for which he is noted. "Writing plays is what I do," he is saying. "Theater is my 'calling,' my profession."

These first brushes with live theater and his discovery that he himself could create that "magic" were revelations to Wilson, seminal experiences in a career that began in 1962 and now extends over nearly a quarter of a century. Any reckoning of the finest talent currently at work in American theater—a list that would include David Mamet, David Rabe, and Sam Shepard—might arguably be headed by his name. Wilson has written forty or more plays, several of which have demonstrated in numerous productions and in recent revivals that they are an enduring part of midcentury American drama. Writing in 1979, one of the *New York Times* critics pronounced him "one of our most gifted playwrights," and more recently another *Times* critic described him as "a persuasive heir to Tennessee Williams." One of Wilson's younger colleagues, David Mamet, has singled him out as "the contemporary playwright I admire the most." Certainly, his "call" to create "magic" in the theater has been sufficiently authenticated.[4]

Lanford Wilson, born in Lebanon, Missouri, in 1937, is the only child of Ralph and Violetta Wilson. His parents were divorced when he was five, and he and his mother moved to Springfield, where she found employment in a garment factory. As a boy visiting her at work, he would "sit on the sewing machine and watch the girls on the line . . . or watch the men on the cutting machines."[5] Four decades later, the playwright drew on these early years for *Talley & Son.*

After six years in Springfield, his mother married W. E. Lenhard and moved with her son to Lenhard's farm near Ozark, where Lanford lived until he graduated from high school in 1955. His father remarried and moved to California after the divorce. *Lemon Sky,* Wilson's most autobiographical play, is about the son's move to San Diego in 1956 when he went to live with his father. While there, he worked at an aircraft plant and attended San Diego State College. Some of his college friends "at State" are characters in *The Sand Castle.* But he and his father did not get on well, and the next year, Wilson moved to Chicago, where he stayed for nearly six years.

After a series of odd jobs in the Windy City, Wilson worked as a graphic artist for an advertising agency, for he had been interested in art almost as long as in writing. Although he studied art and art history at San Diego State, he had decided by the end of the 1950s that a career in art was not for him. About this time he realized that the short stories he had been writing for so many years would really work better as plays. The dialogue had always been better in the stories than the narrative; it was in fact, "so real that the narrative looked stupid and stiff compared to the dialogue." But when dialogue stood alone, "it was something that I had under control and had always been attracted to—juxtaposed sounds and rhythms of characters—and so it was really natural."[6]

The young would-be dramatist was far from satisfied with these first plays, so he enrolled in a play-writing course at a University of Chicago extension. One of these early apprentice pieces, *Miss Williams: A Turn,* was "a silly little sketch I wrote for the Second City [Chicago's famous improvisatory theater group] and didn't have enough nerve to send . . . them." It remained unstaged until 1965, when New York's La Mama Experimental Theater Club was arranging a benefit to help resolve a financial crisis. A number of Off-Off-Broadway playwrights were invited to contribute something new to a marathon evening of very short, three-to-five-minute works. Because Wilson was not in New York during the planning, he was invited at the last minute. Since there was no time to write something new, he went "into the trunk" and came up with *Miss Williams.* Running three minutes with only three characters, the piece concerns Miss Williams, who produces the sunrises over New York City. On the morning in question, she awakens with a hangover only to face a special problem: an eclipse is scheduled. The La Mama production, he says, turned out to be "wonderfully successful, marvelously funny."[7]

In the summer of 1962, Wilson left Chicago and moved to New York City where once again he held a series of odd jobs while living in the Greenwhich Village area. At this point, another very important encounter took place. One evening Wilson went into the Caffe Cino in the Village area and by chance saw a production of Eugene Ionesco's *The Lesson,* one of the seminal plays in the theatre of the absurd movement. Recalling the experience later, he says simply that it "threw me for a loop. It was the funniest play I'd ever seen in my life and serious at the same time."[8] The apprentice playwright was particularly struck to find that serious plays might also be very funny, and some of the "absurdity" of Ionesco's work "rubbed off" on his own early short plays, for example, *Home Free* and *The Madness of Lady Bright.*

Joe Cino (along with Ellen Stewart, the doyenne of the still vital La Mama) was one of the most colorful and important figures in the Off-Off-Broadway theater movement. In December 1958, Cino had started a small coffeehouse, the Caffe Cino, at 31 Cornelia Street, in a small, narrow room with very high ceilings, which was "dark, smoky, cluttered and dirty." Some months after Wilson saw the Ionesco play there in January 1963, he handed Joe Cino a copy of a one-act play called *So Long at the Fair.* With Wilson's involvement, the Caffe Cino truly became a theater, for he introduced "an excellence of production and writing that led to recognition by the critics, first the *Village Voice* and then the other papers."[9]

So Long at the Fair, Wilson's very first production, is unusual in its genesis; it was inspired by a *New Yorker* cartoon of a young man sitting in his studio with paints and easel, music and musical instruments, an unfinished piece of sculpture, and other evidence of artistic endeavor. He has tried them all, only to discover he has talent for none. With the cartoon as a point of departure, and employing two old ballads as musical commentary, Wilson created a young man, Johnny, who has come to New York to be an artist but who has no talent and has failed at everything he has tried. With only a part-time job at a dry-cleaning establishment, he considers returning home to a girl friend, Clementine, but he has caught the eye of the boss's daughter. Attempting to seduce him, she opens up the sofa bed and sprawls all over it. Resisting, he closes her up in it and replaces the pillows, singing "O, my darling Clementine." When the phone rings, he answers it: "Lucy, it's for you." The play ends with a tableau and a woman's voice singing, "Oh, dear, what can the matter be, / Johnny's so long at the fair." Images of entrapment abound, and the young man, Wilson suggests, winds up as "an assistant manager of the biggest dry-cleaning chain in the country."[10]

The script for the play as it was given is now lost, although Wilson believes he may still have the first draft from which he and the director worked. The whole thing was "a horrible experience." His director "just questioned every single line," telling him to "make it clear." In the course of getting the play on the stage, it was largely rewritten and changed completely. Even so, there were "some wonderful things in the script as it was finally done." Looking back, Wilson recalls with amusement that, as far as he and those involved could determine, this little play was the first in which the word *fuck* was spoken on the stage.[11]

At least nine other plays by Wilson, all one-act, were produced at the Caffe Cino. When Joe Cino died two days after attempting suicide in 1967, friends and associates tried to keep his coffeehouse open, adhering to the schedule the owner-manager had planned before his death. The current bill was Wilson's *Lady Bright,* revived again nearly three years after its premiere in that same small, dark room. When the theater finally closed forever, after receiving "1250 police violations in one day,"[12] *Lady Bright* had run a total of 205 performances, and Off-Off-Broadway had begun to change, becoming "less communal, more competitive."[13]

While many of Wilson's one-act plays were being produced at the Caffe Cino, Ellen Stewart's La Mama Experimental Theater Club had provided a forum for his early full-length plays, which demanded larger casts and more elaborate productions. These included *Balm in Gilead* and *The Rimers of Eldritch.* As the playwright began to write longer plays, some had premieres outside New York City: *The Gingham Dog* and *Serenading Louie* at the Washington Theater Club in Washington, D.C., and *Lemon Sky* at the Studio Arena Theatre in Buffalo. The first and third eventually came to Broadway, and while both were received respectfully by the critics, *The Gingham Dog* closed after five performances and *Lemon Sky* after seventeen. *Serenading Louie* did not get to New York until 1976 and then Off-Broadway in a revised version.

If Broadway did not treat Wilson kindly in these first ventures, 1969 still proved to be a landmark year, both for him professionally and for the Off-Broadway theater as well. He and three friends, who had worked together since 1965 and who had common roots in the Off-Off-Broadway theater, were invited to organize a permanent repertory theater by Harry H. Lerner, the founder and acting president of the Council for International Recreation, Culture, and Lifelong Education, Inc. The previous year, two of the four, Marshall W. Mason and Rob Thirkield, had taken a double bill of Wilson plays *(Home Free* and *Lady Bright)* to London under the aegis of the American Theater Project. These two, plus Wilson and actress Tanya Berezin, organized the Circle Repertory Company, named after the acronym of the patron's organization. A nonprofit, institutional theater, the Circle Rep's stated goal was and remains "to establish an ongoing ensemble of artists . . . who would work together to create a living play."

After a hiatus of nearly a year and a half when he had "an incredible writer's block" after the financial failure of *Lemon Sky*, Wilson rebounded, first with short works and, in 1973, with the prize-winning *The Hot-1 Baltimore*. In the next dozen years, he authored five full-length plays, four of one-act, two major television plays, one opera libretto, and one translation of a classical Russian play. In the late autumn and early winter of 1985, he had three major revivals Off-Broadway—of *Lemon Sky*, *Talley & Son* (*A Tale Told* much revised) and *The Mound Builders*—within a two-month period. He and two other founders of the Circle Rep are still extremely active in the company they formed nearly two decades ago. With only rare exceptions, most premieres of Wilson's work since 1971 have been given by this group, which collectively has garnered ninety-seven major awards, including two Tony Awards, a Pulitzer Prize (for *Talley's Folly*), and three New York Drama Critics Circle Awards.

Late in 1985, on the playwright's desk at Circle Rep headquarters lay a copy of his first entirely new work in three years: *Burn This*, scheduled for production during the 1986–87 season.

Chapter Two
One-Act Plays: 1963–1964

Home Free

Although *So Long at the Fair* had been produced in August 1963 at the Caffe Cino, *Home Free* was written earlier, and it is Wilson's earliest published work. It is a two-character play that seems to involve at least twice as many characters, so rich is the imagination that fleshes out a fragile story line. The basic situation of *Home Free* is the trite one of a young couple, expecting their first baby, who are fearful they may be evicted from their extremely modest walk-up apartment in New York City because the landlady does not allow children. This commonplace situation is transformed by Wilson's treatment, however, for Lawrence and Joanna Brown are not married; they are brother and sister, and she is six months pregnant by him. The neighbors, they think, are becoming suspicious of their obviously incestuous arrangement.

In addition, Lawrence and Joanna have created two imaginary characters, Claypone and Edna, whom they view as adopted children and whom they browbeat, tease, cajole, and generally dominate for their own satisfaction. Claypone is "a forty-three-year-old imbecile," an imaginary alter ego and a grotesque reflection of Lawrence. Joanna imagines Edna, who is eight to ten years old, as a younger self ("You can't say things that I wouldn't have said when I was a little girl. You might grow up to be different than me").[1] At the end of the play, illusion confronts reality in the manner of Pirandello when Lawrence sends the imaginary Edna for a doctor as Joanna lies unconscious and dying.

Lawrence, the weaker of the two, fantasizes that he is a scientist or engineer in his opening monologue as he "instructs" Claypone and Edna in Astronomy 101. Evidently he never or rarely leaves the apartment, for he has a fear of the world outside, which Joanna seems to encourage. This fear is projected both onto and through the imaginary Claypone: "They'd grab you and lock you in jail in a minute," Lawrence tells his imaginary pupil (96). His fear of the outside is coupled with his dislike of children. "You have no business being a father at all," Joanna tells her brother, "if you hate children" (104). Although he insists that it is the noise he hates, he calmly imagines that the child she is carrying will certainly be "deformed a little" (103).

Joanna has a stronger grasp on reality, and their fantasy world is one she enters and leaves casually. Her encounters with the outside— her "adventures"—provide excitement in their otherwise shuttered existence. She creates tension with her insistence that their landlady (nicknamed Pruneface) has followed her and may be listening at the door, or that their grocer (Mr. Fishface) guesses their incestuous relationship. She frightens Lawrence with the landlady's threat to make them move because of the noise and mess of a child. "They're afraid of the baby, don't you know that?" she tells him. "They don't want the pain" (100). Her own fear of childbirth is suggested here, which, coupled with his hatred of children and fear of the outside, is nothing less than their rejection of life itself. They live behind a façade of verbal games, role playing, and imaginary companions.

Joanna's attack at the end of the play may be the pains of premature birth. She likes to think, however, she is exceptional because she was a "blue baby," and this, coupled with pains in her shoulder, may suggest she is having a heart attack. (She complains several times of her heart pounding.) She frantically urges Lawrence to go for a doctor and then collapses lifelessly. But he will not go outside, even in a crisis, and "sends" Edna. When he tenderly tries to rouse the unconscious Joanna by showing her the last seat needed to complete a miniature Ferris wheel, it is clear that he is unable to function outside their fantasy world, even though her life depends on it.

Other than the imaginary children, which would seem to owe a great deal to George and Martha's "little bugger" in Edward Albee's *Who's Afraid of Virginia Woolf* (1962), there are three symbols that subtly add dimension to the play. The most important is the miniature Ferris wheel that Lawrence has constructed, and which is complete except for two seats. Besides suggesting the childhood pleasures of a real Ferris wheel, this toy is a metaphor for his attempt to order a world with which he cannot otherwise cope. It is the microcosm of the universe he describes in his opening monologue, a universe that is expanding, a galaxy that is rotating, and stars that are moving at incredible speeds, "every one getting farther from the others" (95). The Ferris wheel lends order to life by offering only two possibilities: either to be kept on it via the force of gravity or to be thrown off. The wheel is a paradigm for Lawrence and his delicate balance between fantasy and reality.

A second symbol is a colorful box with a decorated lid, the Surprise Box, in which Lawrence and Joanna surreptitiously place gifts with which they "surprise" each other. On her return from the store, she hides a pen for him to find; without her noticing, he places a seat for the Ferris wheel in the box. The Surprise Box is a means of controlling astonishment and delight in an environment so carefully ordered in other respects. It is protection against the unpleasant surprises of real life.

Finally, there is the cat imagery. Two cats, one dead and one alive, both somehow relate to the two characters, and the dead cat has something to do with the title. On Joanna's return from the store, she tells Lawrence she has seen a multicolored cat who would not come when she called it. It was fearful (like Lawrence) and pregnant (like her). She has also seen a dead cat. "Why didn't you get it?!" says Lawrence. "You should have brought it home free" (106). This is the only time the title occurs in the play, and although its meaning is vague here—it may echo some childhood game when a runner got "home free"—it may suggest the release of death, a release from a world habitable only through a retreat into the fantasy and illusion of animals and imaginary children.

Home Free is very subtle with its rich texture of images. Like many of Wilson's early plays, its strength lies in the playwright's sympathetic depiction of characters at odds with the roles in which life has cast them, misfits, people in uncertain and fearful conflict with a world that is too much with them. It is funny, yet terrifying portrait of two people who, in a room at the end of their world, elicit our sympathy and interest. The amalgam of possible influences evident here—Williams, Pinter, Beckett, and Albee—shows that Wilson could borrow from the best and mold them all into a vision uniquely his own.

No Trespassing

Home Free was the second and more substantial half of a double bill given at the Caffe Cino in January 1964; the first half was *No Trespassing,* which has never been published. Wilson admits to having written the play a few hours after reading Edward Albee's *The Zoo Story*. It involves a young man who has just killed his weakling father and in his flight encounters a bum to whom he confesses his crime in a somewhat cryptic manner so that the bum does not fully understand the significance of what he is told. Then the younger man allows the bum to pick his pocket. Wilson has admitted that *No Trespassing* was influenced by the Albee play and resembles it.

The Bottle Harp

The Bottle Harp is one of the earliest of Wilson's surviving works that have not been published. It dates from 1963, not long after he came to New York City. Although it does not seem to be autobiographical, it deals with a young midwesterner who comes to New York for the first time on a week's visit to his sister. The play successfully captures a sense of dislocation, expectancy, and discovery that Wilson might have shared with his character who, at twenty-three, is two years younger than the playwright was when he settled in Greenwich Village in 1962. The script needs cutting, but otherwise it contains much that is familiar from other, better-known works of the 1960s. Like many of these one-act plays, *The Bottle Harp* is an exercise in character revelation. Unlike most of Wilson's work of that period, however, it never manages to draw much humor from the characters and their situations, although all three are portrayed with sensitivity and compassion.

Bobby has come from Nebraska to visit his sister, Dorry, five years older, in her small apartment on Central Park West. He had arrived the previous evening, and they have spent the day sight-seeing. Consequently, Dorry is tired and beginning to wonder how to entertain her brother for the rest of his stay. She discusses the problem with her friend, Pat, who is twenty-four and lives down the hall. Pat offers to make dinner for all of them, and Dorry goes out for wine. Bobby seems interested in Pat. When he becomes boyishly aggressive and tries to take her arm for a dance lesson, she first pleads involvement with meal preparations, then fatigue, and finally pushes him away angrily, shouting hysterically, "I don't want you here. . . . I want me and Dorothy to be together! I don't want to be with anyone else. I want to be with her."[2]

At this point, Dorry returns with wine for the dinner, and Pat leaves. The sister admits to her brother that she has been aware of

Pat's attraction to her and was "going to say something" to her friend. She insists she has no sexual interest in Pat but had simply befriended her because the girl was very shy and seemed so alone. She too had been very lonely; she has not made many friends, and she and Bobby have not seen each other for five years.

Although Bobby has shown no great interest in New York City, he suddenly announces that he would like to stay, that there is nothing back in Omaha for him. Dorry says she would like him to remain and offers to share her apartment. Obviously much relieved, she begins to sob, and he comforts her, agreeing that "everybody's lonely." As she cuddles close to him on the studio bed, he begins to tell her a story as he did when they were children.

Several motifs found in *The Bottle Harp* recur in Wilson's plays over the next decade. The reunion of close friends or family members is reworked with more subtlety nearly a decade later in *The Great Nebula in Orion* and the autobiographical *Lemon Sky*. The sterile father-son relationship is analyzed much more fully in *Lemon Sky*. The strong bond between brother and sister had already been given a more "absurdist" treatment in *Home Free*. The subject of homosexuality was being explored in *The Madness of Lady Bright* at about the same time Wilson was working on *Bottle Harp*. Loneliness is the central thematic concern of this character study of three young people who sense their spiritual isolation and the emotional dislocation of life in a large city, which, of course, is also a theme of *Lady Bright* and a problem investigated later and more fully in *The Hot-l Baltimore*.

There are curious gaps and inconsistencies in Bobby's character. He has attended college and knows French and some Spanish; yet he has no interest in reading, and the obvious cultural assets of New York City do not seem to attract him. He does not like Omaha and says he never felt like a Nebraskan. But when he thinks of staying in New York, he has no idea of the kind of job he would like. He is fearful of commitment, even routine, afraid that he will get involved with some kind of work and find himself doing it for the rest of his life.

If, of the two, he seems the one who most lacks direction and goals in life, he also seems to be the stronger. Something had happened earlier in the day that, if interpreted symbolically, suggests a new direction for him. He and Dorry had visited the observation deck of the Empire State Building, and when he leaned through

the bars, his glasses had fallen off. His sister dismisses any incon-
venience this may cause by saying no one in the family wears glasses,
and he had "never cracked a book in his life." Bobby's blinkered
vision may have limited his interests, touristic and otherwise. Perhaps now, without his glasses, he may be able to see his way to a
new life.

Exactly what Dorry does is never clear; probably it is office work.
She does not date much and admits to feeling that "sometimes I
think I'm not doing anything with myself." Pat's social background,
much like Dorry's, is a blur. She does not enjoy people and firmly
tells Bobby she intends to be an old maid: "There are very few old
maids. It's an honorable intention." At the end of the play, she
probably returns to her old status as a lonely outsider.

Certainly a common bond that the brother and sister recognize,
but do not miss, is their father. Alive, happy, and seldom sober
back in Omaha, he is a frequent topic of discussion for his children.
Indeed, he is happier than either of them, but his euphoria is based
on the bottle. "Our dad is kind of a nut," Bobby tells Pat; he is
not only the town drunk but the town clown, and everybody likes
him. His children remember him as always laughing: "his greatest
pleasure is getting drunk; and he gets drunk every day."

Over the years, he has drunk his way through many bottles
containing a wide variety of alcoholic beverages and then used them
to build the "bottle harp" that gives the play its curious title. Around
the family home just outside Omaha, he constructed a fence of
hanging bottles, some suspended nearly six feet off the ground and
some nearly touching it. The bottles do not quite touch one another
as they hang by their individual wires, but when a breeze blows,
they swing together, setting off a tinkling that can be heard for
some distance. He calls this curious construction his "bottle harp,"
but it is, Bobby says, "the biggest and loudest goddamn wind chime
you've ever seen." Instead of being junk, the bottles make a curious
music of the spheres, a quixotic harmony for a man who has found
a life-style through which he can come to terms with life.

And not only do the bottles produce a rough harmony; when the
sun comes up, the light shining through them projects an aureol,
the visual counterpart of music, on the rundown house. The bottles
have been peeled of their labels and polished before hanging. The
father has produced "the only thing we kids will miss at home,"
for he has not been much of a parent. Nevertheless, Pat defends

him: "It isn't everyone that can point to something and say it made them happy."

In addition to showing Wilson's promise, this early play evokes his own recent displacement from the Midwest, as well as his failure to establish a good relationship with his father during his stay in California. But most of all, *The Bottle Harp* conjures up Melvillian isolatoes from the restless generation of the 1960s. It is a compassionate look at "all the lonely people."

The Madness of Lady Bright and Gay Theater

On a very hot, very still summer afternoon in the 1960s, Leslie "Lady" Bright, a forty-year-old "screaming preening queen," slowly goes mad in his small apartment on Manhattan's Upper West Side. This very brief synopsis of *The Madness of Lady Bright* belies not only the complexity of the small tragedy it outlines but also Wilson's mastery of the one-act play. The artistic maturity at which he had arrived after his years of apprenticeship is immediately apparent in this short work, one of his most famous and certainly one of his best. For *Lady Bright* has an enduring originality, even though it depends on familiar material and techniques. It is a highly theatrical, grotesquely comic study of loneliness that is sobering in its universally tragic implications. We laugh at Leslie Bright, for he is very funny and knows he is, but at the same time, we know his solitary state is akin to our own spiritual isolation.

The figure of the homosexual as broadly comic, pathetically tragic—or both—came into its own on the American stage in the 1960s. William Hoffman, in his admirable essay on the advent of gay theater in the 1960s, suggests there were two factors that contributed to the explicit treatment of homosexuality in the theater and the appearance of homosexual characters on the stage.[3] First were the Broadway productions of *A Taste of Honey* (Delaney), *The Hostage* (Behan), and *Inadmissible Evidence* (Osborne), which, because they were British, gave an aura of respectability to homosexual subject matter and proved that the theme was not necessarily taboo to the conservative theatergoers on 45th Street. The second factor Hoffman singles out was undoubtedly the more important: the growth of Off-Off-Broadway in the late 1950s, which had its roots in the fertile climate of the lofts and cafés of Greenwich Village.

The Caffe Cino was, of course, one of these, although not devoted specifically to homosexual plays. But Joe Cino and many of his clientele were gay, so it was natural that both gay plays and plays done in a gay style predominated from the beginning. The group of young writers and actors who worked at the Caffe Cino were "only barely aware that writing about gays was unusual."[4]

The Madness of Lady Bright may well prove to be a classic of the American stage. It was one of Off-Off-Broadway's first big hits, "a landmark in gay plays," Hoffman claims. Leslie Bright would be followed in three years by perhaps the most famous of all gay plays, Mart Crowley's *The Boys in the Band.* Wilson's influence—or his success in creating a character like Lady Bright and finding a public for him—may be seen in the "swishy" Emory of Crowley's highly successful comedy, which "more than any other single play, publicized homosexuals as a minority group."[5]

When Wilson wrote *Lady Bright* in the early 1960s, homosexuality was not a major political issue. That changed in the 1970s, and the play may now be taken as a political statement. How does the playwright feel today, over two decades later, about *Lady Bright?* "If it's taken just as the story of a desperately lonely, rather misplaced person," he has said, "I quite like it. If it's taken as the first homosexual play, I have a feeling that I'm not very fond of it because politically I don't like what it's saying in a vaguely polarized scene. That will pass, I think, and it'll be just the story of a lonely person."[6]

Wilson has always been charmed by the artifice of theater: scenes fading into each other as if by magic; addressing the audience directly; a few actors playing multiple roles; music for background and commentary. All these elements are used to good effect in *Lady Bright.* Although it has three characters, the play is basically a monologue, and it might not be stretching a point to say that most of it is set in the mind of Leslie Bright. (Note that his first name, although more common for males, is also used for females, thus suggesting in another way the sexual ambivalence of the character.)

The one-room apartment is realistically set with the feminine clutter of a very vain "queen." It is also a visual anthology of Lady Bright's love life, for the walls are completely covered with hundreds of autographs—the signatures of past lovers, brief romances, and one-night stands, as well as of two people who really were important to Leslie Bright. The bedroom is almost surrealistic in its record of men who have come and gone, leaving the place a well of loneliness.

Yet, it is easily transformed into a number of other settings: the lighted doorway of a concert hall at intermission, a party scene, the bedroom of heterosexual lovers, and finally a ballroom. Briefly, through dialogue, Wilson creates a variety of settings, real and imaginary, from Lady Bright's past within the small, tawdry bedroom.

Although there are three characters, the play focuses on Lady Bright's forty-five-minute descent into the "madness" of a nervous collapse. For despite the continual presence of the other two nameless characters and the frequent use of the telephone, Leslie is, most of the time, really talking to himself in conversations that are remembered and imagined. Wilson's adroit use of the telephone enlarges the limited world of Lady Bright and recalls in its humor and pathos not only Williams's Amanda *(The Glass Menagerie)*, who sells magazine subscriptions over the phone, but also Blanche DuBois's anxious and frantic calls (in *A Streetcar Named Desire*), as well as the phone-obsessed heroine of Cocteau's *La Voix humaine*.

The two nameless characters, called merely Boy and Girl, are devices to comment on and expedite the action as it moves between present, past, and fantasy. Boy and Girl are occasionally sympathetic but sometimes bored, impatient, and even openly hostile, as they become people Lady Bright has known or encountered briefly. Often they merely echo his words in a disinterested way; chiefly, they are an indifferent and callous chorus:

Girl: [with comic remove] He wants to die, I believe.

Boy: I think that's what he's trying to say.

Girl: Well, it's easy to understand; I mean you couldn't expect him to live like that.

Boy: He's effeminate.

Girl: No one can want to live if they're like that.[7]

They are also variously a pair of irritable lovers, members of a concert audience, and dancers. In addition, the Boy is briefly both Michael Delaney and Adam, Lady Bright's two most memorable lovers, whom he had known a good many years before. Certainly, the Boy and Girl together represent the youth he has lost, the physical beauty he once had, the strength and vigor of twenty years

before, and the early happiness and optimism that have yielded to
loneliness and terror. They are those who "belong," insiders in a
society in which he is an outsider. Most important, all three characters are people in general, all people, in their experience of loneliness and isolation. In their roles as young lovers, the Boy wakes
to find the Girl has left the bed briefly in the night to go out for
some cigarettes: "there was nothing but loneliness," he says. "It's
a terrible thing to wake up to loneliness" (82).

Music furnishes a backdrop for much of the play, an aural atmosphere that functions in a variety of ways: a Mozart concerto
played over a neighborhood radio seems, in its loveliness, to be a
reminder of the beauty of life. A rock-and-roll record sets the tone
for a lively dance scene. Adolphe Adam's music for the ballet *Giselle*
recalls Lady Bright's boast that he can dance like Giselle ("Giselle
was a little willie—a willie is a fairy who dances in the woods").
A Judy Garland recording of "a fast, peppy number" introduces a
scene that culminates in loud "strip music." At least twice, notably
at the climax, all of the musical forms blend into one cacophonous
column of sound, suggesting the emotional breaking point of the
character. The music coming over the neighborhood radios is a
tenuous link with other people; as it comes out of Lady Bright's
phonograph, it is, like the telephone, a mechanical attempt to break
through a wall of loneliness.

The Madness of Lady Bright is a tale of youth left behind, young
love grown old, and innocence and optimism fled. That the lovers
were homosexual is incidental, for the play is in no sense a defense
of a life-style or an attack on it. Homosexuals and homsexual love
are here merely a metaphor for all people and all love. "Some pansies
live a sane life and some don't. Like anyone else," says the boy,
thus making the play a mirror of life in general as well as of one
life in particular (88).

Ludlow Fair

In January 1965, *Ludlow Fair,* a short, two-character play, opened
at the Caffe Cino six days after *Balm in Gilead* premiered at La
Mama. *Ludlow Fair* has more affinities with *Lady Bright* than with
any other early work, although the two-character, female cast an-
ticipates *The Great Nebula in Orion*. In both plays, Wilson is ex-

ploring the empty lives of two women. *Ludlow Fair* is closer to *Lady Bright,* however, in subject matter; one of the women, Rachel, is so preoccupied with a recent broken romance that she half-seriously suspects she is going mad. As with Leslie Bright, the road to madness is paved with the stones of loneliness.

Not much happens in *Ludlow Fair,* which, like *Lady Bright,* is set in a small New York City apartment in the early 1960s. Most of the action has, in fact, already occurred, and we are simply shown Rachel's resulting despair. Sad and bitter, she ponders the wisdom of having dramatically concluded her latest love affair by turning in Joe, her lover, to the police for theft. As it turns out, Joe has also been responsible for other misdemeanors, which come to light after Rachel reports him. The only tension in the play results from her doubts about having turned him in.

Although she forces her roommate, Agnes, to listen to her soul-searching, the focus is not completely on Rachel's latest affair. Agnes is "always nursing someone else's broken heart. Just once I'd like a broken heart of my own."[8] Just as Rachel opens the play with a long monologue, Agnes closes it with her lengthy recollection of a bleak, unromantic past and a realistic assessment of an unpromising future. *Ludlow Fair* does not depend on plot but on a gradual revelation of two banal lives that, although utterly commonplace, are engrossing since they illustrate the universal longing for love fulfilled and loneliness assuaged.

Wilson has admitted that he "had monologue on the mind" while writing the short plays of the early 1960s. This concern with a single speaker is apparent in *Ludlow Fair,* for under the guise of occasionally addressing Agnes, Rachel delivers an extended monologue, revealing her fear and anxiety. She is genuinely funny and yet pathetic in her ultimately sane recognition of her position: "You're not nuts, you're just dull," she tells herself (76). She had been in love with Joe, she thinks, but Agnes reminds her that in the six months before Joe, there had been five others in quick succession. While Agnes listens, Rachel slowly talks herself out of the darkness of disappointment into the grey dawn of acceptance.

As Rachel falls asleep, Agnes in a two-page monlogue offers a rambling survey of her present position: a head cold, lunch with an unattractive man, a weight problem, unhappy childhood memories, and dreams of a muscular, Nordic male. As the play ends, she is not even listening to herself as she mechanically applies cold cream to her face. Her future without love and sex is as empty as Rachel's past with her six lovers.

Near the end of the play, Wilson introduces a quotation from the penultimate poem in A. E. Housman's *A Shropshire Lad* (#62, "Terence, this is stupid stuff"). Although this is a poem about the uses of poetry as a defense against the ills that time inevitably brings, its frame of reference is a comparison of the long-range comforts of poetry with the more immediate, if temporary, effects of ale. Terence (the poet-narrator) admits that he has "been to Ludlow fair," and after "pints and quarts of Ludlow beer," the world did not seem such a bad place. But the next morning, "the tale was all a lie." Even as Rachel realizes that her latest love will pass, Agnes emphasizes the repetitive pattern of life ("It'll be exactly the same tomorrow") by quoting from Housman's poem: "The world, it was the old world yet, / I was I, my things were wet" (88). Ludlow Fair then is a poetic metaphor for the lives of the women, particularly Rachel, who has been to her own Ludlow fair and has found nothing especially wonderful about it.

Despite it dependence on two characters, *Ludlow Fair* is completely realistic in technique. As a study of two lonely people for whom love is either evasive or absent altogether, it is quite effective. Only in one minor respect do the characters fail to ring true: nothing we learn about these women and their lives suggests that they are culturally aware or intellectually sophisticated. Yet, they are both familiar with the Housman poem, and Agnes also makes a casual, joking reference to the "Burghers of Calais," which indicates a passing acquaintance with either Froissart or Rodin, or both. Wilson says he based Agnes's character on a girl he knew who attended Hunter College. Despite the literary references, on suspects that a character like Agnes would not have spent much time in Hunter classrooms.

Chapter Three
Balm in Gilead

In the spring of 1984, twenty years after completing *Balm in Gilead*, Lanford Wilson went back to the Upper West Side of New York City to revisit the neighborhood that was the play's setting. *Balm* was originally presented by the Cafe La Mama early in 1965; in May 1984, a highly acclaimed revival marked its twentieth anniversary. The play, Wilson said, was based on "his experiences in a rundown hotel at 76th Street and Broadway and the coffee shop on its ground floor." The neighborhood was populated by "lots of junkies and drag queens, especially late at night. As a kind of innocent from Chicago, it was alarming to me at first."[1] Twenty years later the coffee shop, which in the play was the source of a bitter and ironic "balm"—a mixture of sex, alcohol, and drugs— had become a grocery store dispensing daily bread to a relatively sophisticated neighborhood.

"A Real Needle Park Then"

The large cast of *Balm in Gilead* constitutes a fairly representative cross section of the nocturnal street people who inhabited upper Broadway in the early and middle 1960s. "They are the riffraff, the bums, the petty thieves, the scum, the lost, the desperate, the dispossessed, the cool," Wilson writes of his characters; "depending on one's attitude there are a hundred names that could describe them."[2] More specifically, they are hoods, whores, pimps, junkies, hustlers, lesbians, addicts, and transvestites. Only two or perhaps three of the characters might conceivably be described as "leads." Joe is a young street-wise New Yorker, newly arrived to the dangerous business of drug-pushing. Darlene, "honest and romantic to a fault," is a recent arrival from the Midwest who is slowly edging her way into the ranks of professional prostitutes. Dopey, an addict, is the most important of several characters who address the audience.

Wilson gives more attention to describing the set, the ambiance, the characters, and even the staging of this play than to any other except *The Hot-l Baltimore,* his better-known "hotel" play. Although *Balm* is set in a small "greasy-spoon" café, it is still in the tradition of the hotel/bar/restaurant play, a terrain Wilson would explore before turning to the front porches of Middle America.

The dramatic ancestry of Wilson's small-time crooks and immoralists is as distinguished and honorable as his characters are deficient in these qualities. Audiences of English drama have always been fascinated by the rogue citizens in Shakespeare's *Henry IV.* John Gay's underworld in *The Beggar's Opera* is still recognizable and entertaining. But *Balm in Gilead* has more in common with such twentieth-century works as Maxim Gorki's *The Lower Depths* and the American drama modeled on it, Eugene O'Neill's *The Iceman Cometh.* In the milieu of a flophouse/bar for down-and-outers, both plays examine the weak and the criminal, people unable to deal with reality except through dreams or alcohol. The customers of Wilson's Broadway café, except Darlene, do little dreaming; they have drugs and sex to alleviate their emptiness. The humor, optimism, and even courage of the characters brighten what could easily be a dark and tragic mood. In this respect, they are reminiscent of William Saroyan's barflies in *The Time of Your Life.*

Plot: Girl Loses Boy

The plot of *Balm* is negligible. As Wilson himself writes, "Much of the play consists of several simultaneous conversations in various groups with dialogue either overlapping or interlocking (5). These conversations ebb and flow and recur with little or no focus or linear development. The principal plotline or unifying narrative involves the brief romance of Joe Conroy and Darlene. A novice at the drug-pushing game, Joe is in trouble because he cannot make payment to the dealer from whom he gets his supply of drugs. Darlene, the character one finally comes to know best, is a vulnerable newcomer to the Big (if wormy) Apple in flight from a failed romance in Chicago. The two meet in the café and retire to make love in her small bedroom across the street. In act 2, they meet again, and Joe is killed by a henchman of Chuckles, the drug dealer (who never appears) on whom Joe has reneged, having decided to get out of the business.

The other characters are revealed more through repeated exposure than through dramatic development. *Balm* depends not on suspense

or even on character revelation but on the director's ability to or-
chestrate twenty-five actors (plus four singers and four children) into
a symphony of sound that is brutally realistic and throbbing with
the excitement of lives lived slightly beyond the edge of desperation.

"Some Common Center"

The challenge of directing and staging a play like *Balm in Gilead*
is a director's nightmare or dream. Wilson has provided very general
instructions that are difficult to visualize merely from reading. The
café setting is suggested by a counter, stools, and a row of booths,
plus "some indication" of a serving area with equipment behind the
counter and a "skeletal indication of a front door and large front
window" (3). Moreover, this set must be constructed so that it can
be picked up easily by the actors and turned "as a turntable would"
until it is facing the opposite direction, that is, with the back of
the set towards the audience. This maneuver is executed by the
actors near the end of act 1 (appropriately as a round is being sung);
at the end of act 2, the set is lifted again and returned to its original
position. In this way, the cyclical nature of events is emphasized,
the sheer repetition inherent in the lives of the characters. Despite
a highly dramatic climax (Joe's killing, which is enacted three times),
everything is very much the same at the end of the play, except
that Joe is dead and Darlene is once again alone. To underline the
cycle of sameness, the monotony of events, she tiredly and sadly
repeats (in the last speech of the play) a line from her very long
monologue that might be half-prayer and half-lament: "Christ, aren't
we even moving?" (72).

The answer is no, not in any truly significant way. They are all
like the trapped souls in Dante's second circle of Hell, swept 360
degrees on the winds of desire. "Everything seems to move in a
circle," Wilson writes in the notes for the play. Within a general
pattern, his people are separate characters with separate goals, "but
together they constitute a whole, revolving around some common
center" (3). And although Wilson does not name the "center," it
is presumably the symbolic qualities of the café as a place of light
for these wounded, fluttering moths: a source of drugs, sex, food,
drink, warmth, and companionship—and sometimes death. The
lighted café-center is the daytime of the long, dark night of their
souls, the "reality" they acknowledge in contrast with the darker

reality of their drab lives. And like their lives, the pace of the play is, for the most part, very rapid—"breakneck fast," says the playwright (5).

Music is more integral to *Balm in Gilead* than to anything else Wilson has written. There is, for example, a quartet of Negro "entertainers" who preface the play with a rock-and-roll song and "with much clapping, dancing, etc. They are accompanied by a typical clangy, catchy instrumentation" (7). This group is heard six more times throughout the two acts, and it is they who introduce the folk hymn "Balm in Gilead," which furnishes the title of the play. In addition to the quartet, a group of minor characters (Bob, Rake, and Tim) plus Dopey sing a "round" that is a lighthearted description of the pointless and empty activities of the hangers-on at the café. Called "Men on the Corner," it is, as they say, "about us. . . . This is our song about us" (40). And like much else in the play, the round is repeated in act 2.

Several other highly theatrical devices are employed in *Balm* with far more flamboyance than in anything written thus far by the young dramatist. At several points, the lights dim, and a spot is directed on one or two characters, usually Joe, to emphasize his importance or to highlight a particular moment (e.g., his murder). There is overlapping or layered dialogue in many scenes, perhaps with as many as three or four conversations or "areas" of action occurring simultaneously. There are brief asides to the audience as well as some unusually long speeches (Dopey, Rake, Fick, Darlene, and Ann), all of which are very significant thematically for the play. Occasionally a character (e.g., Judy) acts as stage director by "directing" other characters who shift scenery ("get that table out of the way, come on; line them [booths] up a little" [7]). Dialogue and action are repeated: Fick says to Dopey, "Hey, ain't we seen this once?" and Dopey answers him, "It's important" (65). At the end of act 1, Dopey, the most important choric character, tells the audience, "We'll call an intermission here" (46). In such a free-form approach, the audience easily comes to accept a role in the action.

The time scheme of *Balm* probably carries more significance for a careful reader than for a live audience. It is clearly a "winter's tale" that Wilson is telling. Fick repeatedly worries about being cold and frostbitten. His desire for protection from the elements extends to a desire for protection from nameless enemies who, like the weather, may lie in wait for him and abuse him.

The play begins in mid-October. By act 2, several days have passed, and it is Halloween, signified by black and orange streamers, a dime-store skeleton (an obvious foreshadowing of death), and a pumpkin. In the scene of Joe's murder, four children wearing Halloween masks beg for trick or treat, contributing a nightmarish quality to the killing that is intensified by its triple enactment. The last moments of the play capture the sterility of winter as Darlene sits silently while Joe's body is removed. Fick comments on the cold as Dopey and Rake repeat fragments of dialogue from an earlier scene. It is a melancholy coda to a street symphony.

"Is There No Balm in Gilead; Is There No Physician There?"

"Balm in Gilead," a famous old Protestant hymn, is traditionally part of the cultural heritage of small-town and rural Bible-belt Baptists, the religious background of Lanford Wilson's first eighteen years. It is sung twice during act 2 of the play, but otherwise there is no reference to it, and certainly there are no characters whose souls undergo anything like spiritual regeneration. Nevertheless, Wilson allows his characters to introduce the concept of a healing balm into the play in a more subtle way. Early in the action, Tig, one of the male prostitutes, announces to Ernesto, a Columbian male prostitute, that "in Egypt they had salves and things that could cure anything" (20). Then he tells John, the counterman, that "they had embalming fluid back then" (i.e., in biblical times) (21). Since Tig is obviously no serious student of the Bible, this may be the playwright's way of insinuating the idea of healing balm as contrasted with that which "embalms," alcohol or drugs, thus causing a kind of death-in-life (exemplified here by the character named Babe).

Anyone who takes note of the words of the hymn must recognize, however, that the dramatist is commenting on the dearth of spiritual values in this small wasteland of prostitutes and addicts. Ancient Gilead, a part of the territory God promised to the Israelites, was famous for its healing balm. Wilson may have had in mind two references to Gilead in the Book of Jeremiah authored by the Old Testament prophet who ceaselessly urged Israel to repent of its worship of idols, prophesying retribution in the final victory of Babylon over Jerusalem and the Jews. In 8:22, Jeremiah speaks of the desolation of the Jews as though it had, in fact, already occurred, still holding out, however, the hope of salvation through a return to God: "Is there no balm in Gilead," he asks. "Is there no physician there?" "Go up into Gilead, and take balm," he instructs (46:11); "in vain shalt thou use many medicines; for thou shalt not be cured."

The title of the play is highly ironic. These lost souls, like ancient Israel, are unable to recognize or accept true "balm"; they worship the false gods of alcohol, drugs, and illicit or deviate sex. By contrasting the spiritual sterility of his characters with the riches and rewards of an Old Testament faith in Jehovah, Wilson (not unlike T. S. Eliot in *The Waste Land*) is commenting on twentieth-century religious malaise. For the characters in Wilson's Broadway café, there is neither balm nor recollection of Gilead, only briefly and partially remembered fragments that they clumsily shore against their ruin.

But this does not mean that Wilson is composing a jeremiad to or about these denizens of the Broadway netherworld. On the contrary, he views his collection of misfits not just realistically but also kindly and occasionally affectionately. He knows what they are, and to some degree he himself is one of them: like Darlene, he had just arrived, "a kind of innocent" from Chicago; unlike Darlene, he is neither stupid nor "romantic to a fault." Wilson is, in fact, the minor character Tim, who is trying to teach Carlo, a Colombian, how to count in English. It is appropriate that these two, who have no special identification in the play, provide literally, in their teacher-student roles, a countdown to Joe's murder. The only truly positive action occurs at the end when Tim finally succeeds in getting Carlo to pronounce correctly the numbers one through ten, a small victory on a battlefield strewn with casualties.

Although there may be no spiritual balm of the biblical type for Wilson's motley collection, they settle for what is available, pseudo-balm in the form of sex, drugs, alcohol, or just companionship and conversation. In one of the key speeches of the play, Dopey talks about the prostitutes and their "johns," insisting that "these girls aren't getting so much exploited because they need these guys. . . . They want someone familiar. You know—to know somebody's touch or their manner or like the texture of his skin" (25). The prostitutes are synonymous in their need with all of Wilson's lost customers at the Broadway café who fend off madness and despair by moving aimlessly in circles, searching for "johns" or just companions. Fick, says Wilson, "will talk to anything that moves" (7).

A slightly different view of these characters may be seen in Dopey's long and important speech. He remembers a comment Darlene had made about cockroaches, and in an extended complaint he recalls that archaeologists in Egypt (perhaps the first clue in Wilson's work that he is interested in that field) had discovered that cockroaches had been around "for about a million years before we came along." And more: the cockroaches can stand *"fourteen times* as much radio-whatever-it-is, you know-activity as we can." So after humanity has destroyed itself, "those same goddamn cockroaches will be still crawling around happy as you please over the ruins of everything (26–27).

The cockroach is clearly a survivor. And so, it seems, are their human equivalents, the habitués of Wilson's cafe. And for their courage and persistence in confronting life in the lower depths of human society, for their sheer ability to *endure,* they have the play-wright's respect. One feels that the young author of *Balm in Gilead* would probably agree with Tennessee Williams's Hannah in *The Night of the Iguana:* "Nothing human disgusts me unless it's unkind, violent."

Chapter Four

Writing about Home

This Is the Rill Speaking

Although *This Is the Rill Speaking* was not written for the Caffe Cino, it premiered there in July 1965. By that time, Wilson had had half a dozen plays produced, and he was deliberately using the form of the one-act play to experiment and break new ground. *Rill,* he says, was an attempt to write about the country and about home, and the same is true of *The Rimers of Eldritch.*

Rill is a work of considerable refinement, highly poetic in structure and dialogue, and altogether charming. It is a portrait of a small Missouri town and its inhabitants, a slice of Americana that features a family on its front porch, two neighbors on their front porch, and eleven other characters in a variety of small-town and rural settings.

Like Dylan Thomas's nostalgic reminiscence, *Under Milk Wood* (1954), *Rill* is a montage of scenes, some lasting a few minutes and others merely vignettes of a few lines. The time is the 1950s. In one scene we are told it is July, but in another, school is still in session, which would suggest May. Several scenes take place on a Saturday afternoon and evening. But the time was probably meant to remain rather generalized with the action of the play occurring over several weeks.

The setting is an "elevated porch with a white railing,"[1] a common feature of almost every small-town and rural home in the Midwest. There are porch steps, some chairs, and a swing. Since the playwright indicates some actions may be pantomimed, certain details of the setting (e.g., a window) may be left to the imagination.

Anyone familiar with the part of Missouri where Wilson grew up would know that *Rill* is set in the playwright's hometown of Ozark. His characters mention Springfield and small towns in the area such as Nixa and Rogersville. Harper's Hill, a local "parking place" for young people, offers a sweeping view of the town of Ozark and is, in fact, the real site of the fictional Talley mansion. Wilson wrote the play for six voices, all of whom speak in "moderately strong Ozark accents" (102), and the dialogue, rhythms, and syntax are consistent with Southwest Missouri speech.

Rill's plot is not strong, and the narrative line is barely discernible. In its montagelike shifting from one group of characters to another, the play might be called impressionistic. As *Rill* begins, the day and the week draw to a close for the Atkins family of four: Mother, Father, teenage Judy, and her younger brother, Willy. The mother and children comment on the emptiness and repetitive nature of the lives of some of their neighbors. Willy is intrigued with the demolition of an old railroad bridge, both a theme (the destruction of the past) and a subject (the decline of the American railroad) that Wilson develops in *The Hot-l Baltimore.*

Willy and a friend consider the mysteries of masturbation. Judy and her boyfriend, Keith, discuss a "town character" named Skelly Mannor who turns up in a pivotal role in *The Rimers of Eldritch.* A typical scene around the Atkins dinner table ("You eat that, young man") concludes as Martha, a neighbor, is heard singing a lullabye: "Hush little baby, don't say a word, / Mama's gonna buy you a mockin' bird" (110). Snatches of this old song recur at least twice later and are ironic comments on birth, the promises of life, and the disappointments it brings.

A scene involving three teenage boys, sick from too much liquor or beer, rounds out a view of life as lived one summer Saturday night in the Midwest thirty or forty years ago. Judy Atkins fantasizes about the dream house she will share with Keith, conjuring up interiors that probably owe much to the latest Sears, Roebuck catalog. In another unrelated scene, one of the young drunks and a pal demonstrate their prowess in the local pool hall. Their dialogue is interesting for the way it captures the bravado of two teenagers who are being small-town men of the world.

After Judy and Peggy talk about movies, two nameless farmers gravely discuss the hay crop. Martha's lullabye is heard again, introducing a scene in which Judy's boyfriend, Keith, flirts with Allison, a friend of hers. In the following scene, it is clear he has seduced her; both friend and lover have been faithless.

The climax of the play is one of momentum rather than of summation. The final scene is prefaced by a series of fragments—exclamations, brief questions, and responses—that "flow one immediately after the other, building" (118). Martha, the play's chorus, sings additional lines of the lullabye. Then longer fragments of earlier speeches by Willy, Keith, Mrs. Atkins, and one of the farmers are repeated word for word. It is as if all the previous scenes had coalesced into a symphony of verbal fragments.

In contrast to the play's whirling climax, the final scene is a peaceful, nocturnal coda. From her bed, Judy asks Willy, "Have you decided what you're gonna be? Are you gonna be an artist like you said?" And Willy, from his bed, replies that he is thinking of being a writer for the newspapers. "I thought I might be an artist on the side kinda. And if I write pieces for the paper too, then I could write pieces about *Nature*. And make people *really notice* Nature" (120). One piece, he says, "would be all about here. Only it'd be about the Nature around us all the time and that we never notice. . . . And I'd have a lot of characters and they'd all talk; only they'd all be things in Nature around us all the time. Like it would be a countryside. And the tree would talk and tell all about itself. . . . And the meadow would talk. And the brook would talk like a laugh kinda. . . . And I figure they'd each one have a little speech that they'd just say out directly about themselves like: 'This is the rill speaking over here.' " "What's a rill," asks Judy. "You know, like 'I love thy rocks and rills,' " he replies (121).

It is finally the voice of the rill that is heard in this play. Willy, as a combination of the typical adolescent and budding artist/writer, is an early, somewhat idealized portrait of the playwright. Wilson was, by his late teens and early twenties, both artist and writer, and a love of nature and particularly plant life forms a minor motif in his work. *Rill* is an aural and visual scrapbook. It is time remembered, a historical anthology of life during the Eisenhower years in a town so small it is a mere island on the open sea of memory.

The Rimers of Eldritch

In content, *The Rimers of Eldritch* (1966) might be called Lanford Wilson's *Our Town,* updated and set in a small Missouri Peyton Place, with strong overtones of William Inge's *Picnic* or Tennessee William's *Orpheus Descending.* In dramatic technique, however, it is his *Dream Play.* As in August Strindberg's masterpiece of expressionism, the free-flowing structure of *Rimers* is governed only by the mind and consciousness of the dramatist who, with little regard for chronology, recreates selected fragments of life in a small Missouri town in the 1950s.

In its montage structure, *Rimers* most resembles *This Is the Rill Speaking,* which immediately preceded it. One short scene follows or blends with another, and frequently scenes occur simultaneously. Wilson has conceived the play in such a way that lighting is "the most important single scenic element," for it is the means of focusing on a single character or group of characters and isolating the action in a particular time-space setting. Like *Rill, Rimers* requires a production in which realism is kept to a minimum. The play was originally done at La Mama on "a series of six or eight descending irregular levels," with railings to suggest specific settings, for example, a front porch. But the set may also include "various architectural elements," such as gables, trees, and ruined buildings.[2]

Unlike many of Wilson's early plays in which plot is subservient to character and theme, plot is important in *Rimers.* And although the plot is complicated, it seems more so because the action is fragmented into many small vignettes rearranged in seemingly haphazard fashion within a time frame encompassing six months or more. The climax, with its final revelation of the pervasive effects of evil in a small town, is a highly effective coda.

A synopsis of *Rimers* involves sorting out and putting into chronological order three main plot lines, each of which involves two different families, parts of families, or individuals: (1) the Windrod-Mannor plot in which all three characters are of major importance: Nelly Windrod, the strong-minded, middle-aged woman who owns the local corn mill; Mary, her elderly mother; and Skelly Mannor, the "town hermit"; (2) the Johnson-Groves plot, which concerns farmer Peck Johnson; his wife; their children, Patsy and Josh; and Cora Groves and her young lover, Walter; (3) the Conklin-Jackson plot, which focuses on eighteen-year-old Robert Conklin and fourteen-year-old Eva Jackson.

One summer night, Nelly Windrod shoots and kills Skelly Mannor, a local eccentric and archetypal "outsider." She believes he is attacking two of the town's teenagers, Robert Conklin and Eva Jackson, in the woods behind her house. Her mother, Mary Windrod, witnesses the killing and, although confused at first, soon realizes that Skelly is innocent. However, because she is senile, no one takes her seriously. The other two witnesses, the "victims," insist he is guilty. We learn early in the play (and long before the onstage killing) that Nelly is on trial for murder. Approximately halfway through act 1, we learn of her acquittal. Not until the last minutes of the play do we learn what really happened.

It is interesting that in Wilson's view of small-town life, the family, the basic unit of society, often exists only in fragments. In *Rimers,* the Johnson family of four is the only "complete" family, and it is, in most respects, a typical one. Patsy, sixteen and the "prettiest girl at Centerville High," dates a nice boy whom she forces into marriage at the end of the play because she is pregnant by Walter, a drifter, who is the hired-man/lover of Cora Groves, owner of the Hilltop Cafe. Cora, fair-minded and intelligent, is also vulnerable and passionate. She defends Skelly Mannor as a harmless eccentric and a good worker. She guesses correctly that it was not Skelly who attacked the two young people and privately gets the truth out of Eva. In retaliation, Eva's mother calls her a whore. Cora's involvement with Walter immediately classifies them both as outsiders in the community. When she discovers Walter has left her (because he has impregnated Patsy), she is deeply hurt.

Robert Conklin, eighteen, is a quiet boy who spends his spare time walking in the woods with Eva Jackson, crippled and four years his junior. His older brother, a stock car racer named Driver, had been killed three years before in a crash. Sometimes called Driver Junior, Robert is nothing like his brother. He has no interest in cars or in dating, all of which, plus his association with Eva, makes him seem somewhat "different."

Another of Wilson's outsiders, Eva is passionate, lonely, and fascinated by Robert. On the night Skelly is shot, she baits Robert by implying that he is unable to have sex; he retaliates by attacking her. Through her window, Mary Windrod sees Skelly come to the girl's rescue. Not understanding at first what is happening, she calls Nelly and watches as her daughter shoots the old man.

Following the killing, the play shifts to the courtroom with Robert on the witness stand. He takes the oath and immediately breaks it by swearing (as Eva has already done) that Skelly had chased and then attacked them. We are struck by the ease with which Robert perjures himself, and we realize that he and Eva, despite their youth and seeming innocence, are as deeply infected as the rest by the town's moral malaise. They, like most of the people in Eldritch, are "rimers," for rime is a metaphor for the hypocrisy, the lies, and the loveless passion that pervade the town, a community that has been mined of its humanity and integrity like the moribund land.

The geographical setting of *Rimers* is the south-central area of Missouri where Lanford Wilson grew up. He undoubtedly borrowed the name Eldritch from a small town not far from Lebanon, Missouri, where he was born, and there is a reference to the old Sparta Road, which was not far from Ozark, Missouri, where he lived. But this part of the state is not associated with coal mining. On the other hand, Wilson's Eldritch is located twenty miles from Centerville, presumably Centerville, Iowa, which would place Eldritch in the coal-mining belt of northern Missouri. Wilson has simply combined two localities by borrowing place names and geographical features from the area where he grew up and assigning them to another some distance away (he also does this in *Fifth of July*).

But it is the metaphoric aspects of the setting that are most important. In no other play does Wilson so emphasize the ruin, the sterility, the utterly barren nature of the setting, not even in the ugly cityscape of *Balm in Gilead* or the run-down Hotel Baltimore. Eldritch was "built on coal with coal money and deserted when the coal gave out" (7). The mining people are all gone now; "they raped the land and moved away." With a population of seventy, it is a ghost town, repeatedly described as "evil," "wicked," and "dead."

The ruined condition of the town extends to the surrounding countryside. A chorus of minor characters comments on the weather: the late spring thaw that delayed planting of crops, the heavy rains that caused spring flooding, and a recent dry spell that presages a drought. This brief catalog of unfavorable weather conditions is a subtle commentary on Eldritch as Wilson's "waste land." In T. S. Eliot's terms, the small town is the "objective correlative" of the spiritual condition of the people of Eldritch and, by extension, of the country.

Granting this, certain other features of the plot assume significance in constructing a basic myth for the play. In earlier times, Eldritch enjoyed a pastoral age when the town was a cow pasture, before the coal people came and "raped" the land. It was "a wonderful place" long before Driver Conklin's accident, and "wonderful" is used to describe him. He was "a beautiful man" who "lived so dangerously; like the world wasn't turning fast enough to suit him" (31). He drove through Eldritch "like a big shot," and people "lined up after him in cars, trailing after him and honking like a string of geese coming into town" (30). But three years before (significantly, around Memorial Day), Driver had died in a racing accident, and his twisted car was left in the center of town, a macabre memorial to a local hero and a wasted life.

There was another side to this small-town Adonis. It was generally assumed that he was as successful with women as he was with cars, but Skelly tells Robert that he saw his brother attempting to have sex with a local girl and, failing, abuse her physically while he resorted to masturbation. Despite his reputation as a virile young god, Driver was, in fact, as sterile as the community that championed him.

Skelly, in his youth, embodied some of the qualities that Driver was presumed to have. He had seduced the daughter of the wealthy man who had bought the original Eldritch family place, the symbolic rapist who had then moved away when the mining industry ran dry. That was over forty years before, when the land was still "virginal." That was an age of consummated sex, of fertility, growth, and prosperity. But now Skelly has to live with having committed an act of bestiality with a sheep (for which the local boys "baa" at him), and Driver could not, despite his masculine image as a daredevil racer, complete the sex act. Moreover, Robert, Driver's "nice," younger brother, is finally goaded into the near rape of Eva, and together they perjure themselves to cover up the murder of Skelly, the fallen Adonis of an older generation. In killing him, Nelly Windrod acted with the approval of most of the community, and Skelly, a sacrificial scapegoat, paid with his wasted, eccentric life, a life paralleled by Eldritch itself, fallen from pastoral beauty into ruin and decay.

Thematically, this is a restatement of Wilson's concern with the "tearing down" of America, a theme he admits runs through much of his work. In the largest possible sense, tiny, ruined Eldritch, located in what advertisers call "the heartland of America," is symbolic of the country as a whole: a virgin land, exploited and "raped" by those who live in it and on it. It has become as hollow as its inhabitants. The old—the "rimers," the frost-bringers (*rime* is actually an icy covering on objects), and death-dreamers—taint the young. Those who remain are infected; those who leave suffer from a sense of displacement. Having cut themselves off from the past by their cavalier treatment of their inheritance, they become rootless.

They are from "somewhere else," as they live out their rootlessness in the Hotel Baltimores, Needle Parks, and affluent living rooms of large American cities. *The Rimers of Eldritch* is a bitter indictment of humanity gone to seed in an American Eden.

Chapter Five

One-Act Plays: 1965–1966

The Sand Castle

In 1956, several months after his graduation from high school, Wilson went to California, a visit that furnished material for *Lemon Sky* (1970) and *The Sand Castle,* which was produced by La Mama in 1965. While in California, Wilson attended San Diego State College, and this time at "State" is the basis of *The Sand Castle,* not so much the playwright's experiences as the friends he made there. "Everyone in *Sand Castle* is *directly* from people I went to school with in San Diego," Wilson has said; "those kids and that mother and her story and the whole damn thing—except the bus driver who is a fabrication out of the blue just because he was necessary for some sort of a story." The boy, Owen, is Lawrence of *Home Free,* only "a different side of him."[1] Sasha, the funniest character in *Castle,* is based on the same friend who had been the model for Agnes in *Ludlow Fair.*

The play begins late one Saturday evening in summer when two college students, Calvin and Sasha, visit Irene and her children, two of whom, Owen and Joan, are (like Sasha) students at "State." Clint, a city busdriver, stops by to make a date with Irene for a Sunday morning drive. Irene's third child, young Kenny, reports a cave-in at Sunset Cliffs on the beach not far from their home. Joan contrives to lure Clint back later that evening and seduce him on the beach, so causing a confrontation between mother and daughter. Owen and Calvin quarrel over Jill, Calvin's wife. For the most part, the plot depends, except for the two confrontations, on character revelation. Of the seven characters, Owen and the two college girls, Joan and Sasha, are the most complex and so the most interesting.

Owen, twenty-two, is first seen absorbed in a game of solitaire, which tells something of his introverted nature. He harbors an idealized passion for Jill (unseen), who is pregnant. When Calvin jokes about having affairs with his clients (he takes tourists out on the ocean in his boat) while his wife is pregnant, Owen becomes angry. Pushed by the younger man's outbursts, Calvin tells him his "stupidity is embarrassing" and that he had "better read up" on the sexual aspect of marriage. He warns the younger man not to visit Jill while she is pregnant. When Irene asks her son why he is so jealous of Calvin's relationship with his own wife, Owen's response is even more overwrought: "Jill's the most beautiful thing in the world and she's carrying *life* in her and she's holding in her *body* all—the—*wonder*—and *mystery*—." Joan succinctly sums up her brother's problem: "She's not a love, she's a religion for him."[2] Finally, Owen's melodramatic attack on Calvin and declaration of love for Jill seem much too intense for either the character or the situation.

For the most of the play, Joan, who is twenty, reacts to her mother and two brothers with bored indulgence and occasional irritation. The only explanation for her aggressive behavior toward her mother's middle-aged suitor is her annoyance at their Sunday trip to the mountains. She steals Clint's keys to guarantee he will return later that evening, when she suggests they visit the cave-in at Sunset Cliffs together. Only at the end of the play do we know that Irene has heard Joan's conversation with Clint, which precipitates their confrontation. This disclosure of mother-daughter rivalry is unsatisfying, especially since Irene implies that Joan's successful seduction of Clint has been two years in the making.

Throughout the play, there has been talk of the family's return to Fresno, where they had lived when Owen and Joan were young, before their father, Irene's husband, had been killed in the war. After her argument with her mother, Joan announces she will go to Fresno. "No, you don't even want to," responds Irene. "If you wanted to you would" (49). Owen, too, speaks of a move to Fresno. For this family, however, that city is a world of the past to which they might like to return but cannot.

Sasha, much funnier than her counterpart in *Ludlow Fair,* is the happy-go-lucky coed of the innocent 1950s, recalling with zest her childish pranks in the chemistry and biology labs and flirting extravagantly with Calvin and Clint. But when Calvin pretends to respond to her allure, she warns him that "I may act like a terrible flirt, but I am a very *puritanical young person.* . . . I belong to the Protestant Youth Group, for Christ's sake" (40). Joan accuses Sasha of turning to ice when anyone touches her. Sasha, as Wilson said, is "a little frigid." Since she is not part of the play's focus (the family), Wilson does not probe very deeply into her problems.

Irene is a published poet "in all the little magazines and in a lot of the big ones and books" (18). She also teaches at local writers' conferences, but we never see her in these roles. For the most part, she is an indulgent mother of two college students and a twelve-year-old. She is altogether sympathetic as a middle-aged woman longing for love and companionship, even from Clint, who is clearly not a suitable match. She admits she might consider marriage to him, but her admission to Joan that she loves him is belated and no quite believable.

Clint is every inch a stereotype and "right off the assembly line," as Irene tells him. He is "Marlboro Country and the Camel Man and Randolph Scott. . . . All the things that we're supposed to believe are masculine and red-blooded in the pulp fiction sense" (20). Dramatically, his chief function is to reveal Joan's problem and Irene's emptier hopes.

Calvin seems drawn from life without really being transformed into a character. He is best when "putting on" Sasha and "putting down" Owen. Young Kenny may owe something to Wilson's two stepbrothers whom the playwright may have met for the first time during the visit to California. He is charming when addressing the audience in a prologue and boyishly innocent and curious about his small world.

The most subtle aspect of *Sand Castle* is the symbolism of the setting. The Renolds' family home is the last house on the street in Ocean Beach, a suburb of San Diego. The floor of the house has a light dusting of sand; the front porch is covered with sand; the yard is surrounded by a low wall to keep out sand; the house, says Wilson, should seem "almost to be growing up from the beach" (9). Like its title, the play evokes not only the constructs of childhood, the source of Owen and Joan's maladjustments, but also the present instability of this family of four: Irene has dried up as a writer, and Joan longs for sexual fulfillment, competing for it with her mother. Owen is paralyzed by a love so romantic and idealistic that it verges on the morbid. The family relationships are being eroded by social pressures and the demands of maturity, just as Sunset Cliffs is slowly being undermined by the ocean, itself an inexorable, fatalistic presence "heard distantly throughout the play" (9).

The house built on sand acquires another symbolic dimension, a dire one, in fact, when Calvin repeats the prophecy that "during a violent earthquake the whole state of California would slide off into the Pacific ocean. . . . Sometime around now" (30). Wilson would have been acquainted through his Baptist unbringing with the New Testament parable (Matthew 7:24–27) of the foolish man who built his house on sand where it was destroyed by rains, floods, and winds. This home is no bulwark against the outside world but a "sand castle" stuffed with comic books and unfilled hopes, dreams, and loves.

The fog from the ocean (like the fog that slowly crowds out reality for drug-addicted Mary Tyrone in O'Neill's *Long Day's Journey into Night*) is also symbolic: Owen remembers that he and Jill used to walk in fog "so thick you could hardly see the rocks" (51). And Irene remembers sitting on the shore with her young husband, thinking "how wonderful everything would be," with the fog coming in (like death) around them. For Owen and Irene, the fog symbolizes the romantic basis of their lives, his world of comic books and ideal love and hers of poetry and a sexy busdriver: "We're perpetually young, you and me," she tells him, "but I'm afraid that makes us pretty naive and pretty vulnerable" (51).

Like other early Wilson plays, *The Sand Castle* breaks down the barriers between actors and audience. Young Kenny speaks a prologue ("I get to begin the play now, and I get to close it later on with little narrations" [10]); however, it is typical of the casual structure and "informal" mood that, despite his promise to "close it," he is asleep at the end, and Irene very shyly and apologetically announces, "This is the end of the play" (53). Kenny's speech betrays the young playwright's admiration for Tom in *The Glass Menagerie*. In *Sand Castle,* however, all the actors except Clint address the audience or somehow acknowledge it.

Music is more integral to *The Sand Castle* than to any other Wilson play except *Balm in Gilead,* often to the point of imparting a vaudevillelike mood to the action. "There is a Tavern in the Town" is a theme song and recurring motif (as well as a subtitle for the play). In the quiet conclusion the line "And may the world go well with thee" functions as a poignant farewell, even a benediction, from the actors to the audience, their guests for the evening.

The Sand Castle is not in the front ranks of Wilson's short plays, but it is an immensely likable work by a young man who recalls with nostalgia a year of college and the friends he made, a young playwright skylarking through the dramatic conventions of stage realism and reveling in admitting the audience to a family circle of players. Perhaps *The Sand Castle* is Wilson's first attempt to invent a stage family. In earlier plays, he had created an artificial family consisting of people often described as "misfits." The Renolds family has its problems, but it is and remains a family despite any misfitting. Wilson returned to the family portrait a few years later when he depicted his father's second family in *Lemon Sky*.

Sex Is between Two People and *Days Ahead*

In the autumn of 1965, Wilson was a "playwright observer" in a program for young dramatists and went on the road for the pre-Broadway tryouts of the English thriller *Wait until Dark*. During the weeks in New Haven and Boston, he wrote *Sex Is between Two People* and *Days Ahead*. He promptly turned them over to Neil Flanagan who directed both and acted in *Days Ahead* at the Caffe Cino where they were given as a double bill in December of that year.

Never published, *Sex Is between Two People* is a short sketch, a "dumb little show," Wilson has called it.[3] It deals with two homosexuals who have picked up each other and gone to a private room in a steambath. They are both so timid that they never get around to sex; they sit on the bed and talk about opera and movies, then agree it is time to leave. In their case, sex is *between* two people, separating them; because of it, they never touch literally or figuratively. They might have become good friends, but they part "absolutely appalled with each other." "I parody a stupid movie," Wilson recalls, "the one where they drag that cannon all over Spain" (*The Pride and the Passion*).[4] One of them did not understand the movie, and the other tries to explain it, getting it all wrong. But never this twain shall meet, in love anyway. *Sex Is between Two People* has only been done at the Caffe Cino, and the playwright has the only copy.

Days Ahead, the other half of the bill, is a dramatic monologue, perhaps Wilson's purest attempt at monologue in this period when he admittedly was "hung up" on it. A man, about forty-five, with "the look of a small businessman," hurries breathlessly into a room that, if furnished at all, is furnished with dusty Victoriana.[5] A wall has very obviously been built across the room, cutting it into two halves. The half we see should appear to have been "closed off for a long time, dusty, stale" (65). The only necessary prop is a chair.

In the course of the monologue, the man reveals that twenty years before, he had walled up his wife, Beth, into the other half of the room, promising to visit her once a year and bring her up to date on what had happened to him. This visit, however, is different. He has come a day early, the thirteenth instead of the fourteenth, because he is excited. As he situates his chair very close to the wall, his face not more than a foot from it, he explains that he has had a "revelation." Before describing what was revealed, however, he goes through a small diary, trying to find something in the twelve months that is worth telling her, but he only comes up with banalities about the seasonal changes in the park or the new furnishings of a friend's living room. Clearly, his is an empty, uneventful life.

The "revelation," when he finally comes to it, is simply that, twenty years later, he wants to return to her. "It seems you're always with me lately," he begins, producing a fork (68). Twenty years ago, "some deficiency" in him made him feel "restless, discontent." To prevent arguments and bickering, he had built a partition, walling her behind it. Now he has outlived his restlessness and looks forward to the "days ahead" with her. He admits he may have been wrong to leave her alone, but "the doubts have waned and I love you" (70). Well before this point, he has begun to dig away at the wall with his fork. He continues to reassure her with talk of their bright future as the lights dim and his voice becomes inaudible.

The power of this short piece resides in the horrified fascination with which an audience is caught up in the fantasy of a very mad man who has somehow extended his vision over two decades. The piece recalls Poe's "Cask of Amontillado" or some of Browning's madmen. A little bit of a stunt, *Days Ahead* is ultimately quite limited in both appeal and impact.

Wandering

Like several of the early short plays, *Wandering* was performed at the Caffe Cino (as part of the 1966 Easter show) and was one of the early collaborations between the playwright and Marshall W. Mason who, as the director of so many of Wilson's plays, became a major influence on him. Mason and the author played the two male roles in a cast of three. *Wandering* is brief and skillfully done, based upon one or two familiar themes and technically evoking the absurdist theater so popular in the 1950s and 1960s.

The three characters are He, She, and Him, all of whom are about twenty-five. The only prop is a bench that functions as a variety of furnishings. The acting is supposed to be quite stylized, for the actors are to "retire" to the "attention" position when they are not speaking. Furthermore, actions are pantomimed, and props are imaginary. Except for five pauses near the end, the play is to be performed rapidly. Most of the dialogue is very short lines of just a few words, recalling in its brevity—and once or twice in its wit— certain moments in Pinter plays of about the same period.

In subject, *Wandering* aims at nothing more than a condensation of a man's life. The man is Him; He and She play various roles such as mother/father, army medics, wife, secretary, and potential employer. Him is quickly taken from the age of sixteen to eighteen, when he has to cope with military personnel as the army attempts to draft him, then swiftly into marriage and children, followed by a period of illness and a career, apparently in business. Finally, there is a rather ambiguous period in which Him is described as a "bit of a radical" and "a lost lamb" by She and He, who seem to be his wife and father-in-law.[6]

The one-word title of the play recurs in the dialogue several times: "Wandering" or "I was just wandering," always spoken by Him. It is a metaphor for the progress of everyman through various phases of life. There is, at the end, a recapitulation of the action, with earlier dialogue repeated verbatim, a device Wilson sometimes employed during this phase of his career. This coda is divided by five pauses. Interspersed in the repeated dialogue are lines that are new and provide the thematic point of the play: "that can't be the way people want to spend their lives," says Him (99). After other dialogue, he repeats the line again, and the play ends with his question: "Can it?" (100).

Wandering is a young playwright's questioning of the values of society as exemplified in the lives of the older generation, a familiar motif. He and She are parodies (e.g., of American parents) or stereotypes in their attitudes toward manhood, patriotism, and success, whereas Him does not believe in war or killing, not even for freedom, love, or money. Also familiar here is Wilson's tendency to eradicate time, blend one vignette into another, reduce setting to a bare minimum, and have actors play many characters. *Wandering* is a ten-minute everyman's progress as imagined by a young playwright who admires Thornton Wilder (in works like *The Long Christmas Dinner*) but who also wants to experiment and "keep up" with absurdist times.

Chapter Six
The Gingham Dog

When *The Gingham Dog* opened in New York City in 1969, it was Wilson's first Broadway show, and it ran for a scant five performances after a few previews. When it was revived Off-Broadway in 1981 for a limited run, the *New York Times* critic, in a generally favorable review, described it as "very much a play of the 1960s."[1] That it is. That decade saw the dismantling of tradition and convention in a number of areas, including marriage. *The Gingham Dog* is about an interracial marriage between a black woman from Manhattan and a Kentucky-born white man. Wilson's couple seems to have lived relatively free of the problems one might expect to arise from such a union, at least for a good part of their short marriage, and to have been just two people in love. The play is also of the 1960s in its depiction of the black woman's increasing militancy in racial matters. And it is reminiscent of the social consciousness of the decade in the husband's fashionable commitment to a profession (draftsman and would-be architect) that is dedicated to improving living conditions for minorities.

This is a very political play, typical of its decade. Yet the *Times* reviewer of the 1981 production suggests that the play "has very little to do with 60's politics." Wilson would probably not agree with this, for he has said that he always thinks of his plays as "very political." Assuredly, it is true that he often treats themes that are political in nature, for example, race in this play, the destruction of the national heritage in *The Mound Builders,* and the effect of the Vietnam War in *Fifth of July.* Yet, his plays generally originate in and with a character, and it is out of his characters that the theme develops. It is the universality of both character and theme in *The Gingham Dog,* rather than the contemporary political aspects, that makes the play memorable.

The Gingham Dog is a play about the end of love and the failure of a marriage that seemed to have a lot going for it, even though it has obviously had to face major problems. Considered now in that light, it bears up well a decade and a half later. It is to Wilson's credit, and the play's, that the material hardly seems dated at all; that while it is set in the 1960s, it still manages to transcend the concerns of that turbulent era. *The Gingham Dog* acknowledges that while race is an important aspect of interracial marriage, it is only one aspect; ordinary human concerns and weaknesses are of equal importance. Wilson's couple does not separate entirely because of problems stemming from racial differences. The two have grown apart in the same way, and for some of the same reasons, that a great many couples did in the postwar period. They would not be unique if they were both white or both black, and so they are not unique merely because they are partners in a mixed marriage.

Plot: "Call It Heart Failure."

The plot is one of Wilson's thinnest. There is little action, for this is a play of revelation in which two people, Vincent and Gloria, gradually come to understand and accept that, after three years of marriage, they have already gone their separate ways.

After having spent the last several nights with friends, Vince returns to their East Village apartment on New York's Lower East Side where he is sorting out and packing his share of their possessions. A neighbor, Robert, is the catalyst for a heated exchange with Gloria that reveals her involvement in racial crusades and Vince's resentment of her commitment, which he feels has become an obsession. Vince's younger sister, Barbara, more recently out of Kentucky than he, tries very hard to seem liberal-minded about the breakup of her brother's marriage. But her attempt ends in a vituperative denunciation of Gloria that reveals her hypocrisy and superficiality. After Vincent himself quarrels with Gloria, he leaves; she tries to phone her family in Harlem, only to find that she is totally unable to communicate with them.

If act 1 is a capsule of the arguments, charges, and countercharges of the preceding year, which have brought these two intelligent and sensitive people to the point of separation, act 2 is a quiet, sad farewell to a love that has died. The stage is dimly lighted, and the act is to be played "very, very slowly" with "long wandering pauses."[2] Vince returns, somewhat drunk, to the apartment. Gloria has not slept and has, in fact, brought home a man she met in a bar who remains asleep offstage for the entire act. Most importantly, act 2 is a reckoning in that both people confront squarely, with little help from each other, what really went wrong and what each has become: "You tucked up into your company and I tucked up into a shell," says Gloria (54).

The title of the play comes from a poem, "The Duel," by the immensely popular poet, Eugene Field, who wrote early in the century. In a cheerful fantasy, two stuffed toys, a gingham dog and a calico cat, fight and devour each other in the nursery during the small hours of the night while their young master is asleep. And so it goes with Wilson's couple: they have devoured each other in marriage and must begin new lives.

Vince, the Gingham Dog

Vincent is Kentucky-born, but there is very little about him that suggests the South; Wilson (who is very careful about accents) does not indicate that there is even a vestige of southern speech. Uprooted from his native element, he is, in fact, one of Wilson's displaced characters who has not really managed to settle anywhere. He refers to the possessions—the books, stereo elements, and drawing board—that he is packing to send to storage as "so much crap," "ganglia," and "roots" (14). He makes no distinction between property that would give him a sense of place and identity and the appliances that he has collected in his short marriage.

It soon becomes clear that for Gloria, Vincent's work is the principal sore point. He is a draftsman for a construction company that builds multihousing units to replace slum dwellings. Barbara cannot understand why her sister-in-law is not proud of Vince for "trying to do good at his job." Gloria retorts that his job has nothing to do with good: "Vince is trying to do *well* at his job, which is another thing altogether" (30). When his wife pushes him, Vince will not admit to being proud *of* his work, merely insisting that he does it well and that he is proud of the *way* he works and his loyalty to the company.

He bolsters his pride by insisting that he works "in a very specialized, a very narrow, qualified, exciting area." "Genocide," Gloria charges; "Instant tenements. Add ashes and stir" (31). What he is building, she claims, is a "vast brick ghetto," not much different from those the poor currently live in. When Barbara realizes the new units are located in the Brownsville section of Brooklyn and are for blacks, she is nonplussed at Gloria's attack on her brother and his employers. But when Gloria demands to know if Barbara would like to live—indeed, *would* live—in one of her brother's buildings, Barbara is forced to answer no. Not a person of much depth, not even in Vincent's affectionate view, Barbara, probably for the first time, has been forced into honest objectivity. "I only wanted to show you once that you could think," Gloria tells her sister-in-law and reminds her that neither of them has to defend such moral chicanery just because Vince is a part of it (33).

Vincent is a 1960s variation of Ibsen's master architect, Halvard Solness (Robert jokingly calls him "Master Builder"), for both men in their ambition ignore the human element in their architecture. Vince, of course, is really a minibuilder who has not been able to leave behind the thing he most deplores in his own background: "small people" in "small Southern towns" (38). Yet, his vision of small, sterile apartments for the poor shows that he is, in fact, a victim of the past he tried to escape by moving to New York.

What remains for him in act 2 is to come to terms with his own flaws. And once again his southern background is invoked when he tries to explain to Gloria in the half light of a cold dawn that southerners have "this gimmick, this knack for not understanding something outside of what they accept as right. . . . You just dial into things that you decide are all right. Everything else doesn't exist. I mean whole countries—whole centuries don't exist" (50). He realizes, of course, that it is his "gimmick" too, that this southern "facility" is universal. He has simply excluded from view and conscience the moral compromise involved in producing instant, sterile environments for tenants at his mercy, even as he is only dimly aware of his own equally cold, barren—and now-vacant—apartment.

As the act winds down to its sad, quiet conclusion, Vince considers that he should quit his job. With a job, "You have only your own responsibility—to your company, which is synonymous with yourself, you believe. And any outside responsibility is only a threat." But he realizes that he will probably not quit, that "I don't know how to change now" (55). Someday he will tell them what they are doing, and perhaps they will fire him. "We started getting principles" he tells Gloria; "they take a lot of maintenance" (56). Not really. Vince has mistaken principles for ambition, ambition for commitment. He will have to learn the difference. That he has not is clear, as the play ends slowly and quietly with the agony of two people who loved each other and are only beginning to feel the loss. At dawn there is no promise of reconciliation.

Gloria, the Calico Cat

A grade-school psychologist, Gloria is a "well-educated, if somewhat vulgar, graduate of New York University," charming, energetic, detached from some things but quite passionate about others (5). In the last two years of their marriage, she has become a militant crusader for racial freedom, an issue about which she had evidently not felt so strongly before. The first political exchange in the play not only shows just how far the marriage has deteriorated but also that this issue has driven a wedge between them. Blacks "had empires and temples when you babies were still dirtying up your Alley-Oop underpants," she taunts (17), while Vince resorts to vulgar accusation that blacks ate the missionaries sent to help them. Gloria was a poor Harlem black and is proud of having escaped to a better life, but she carries her militancy in racial matters to the point of masochism.

The central scene of the play is the argument between Vince and Gloria after the two minor characters have left. It is significant because it clarifies the importance of race in their marriage. Here, more than anywhere else in the play, race is understood to be a political issue but only up to a point—the point at which Gloria becomes a "professional Negro" and Vince becomes a company man. "At least," she says, "our breaking up didn't have anything the hell to do with color." "Not directly," he replies. "Not directly or indirectly," she insists. It had to do with "the change in you," Vince charges, and that had to do with color. She used to be a human being, he charges, but in the last two years she has become "a 'Black'; a professional Negro, and I didn't marry a Black" (36). The Gloria he married thought all people were equal, but she has managed to convince herself that she is not equal at all. And this has brought Vince to the point of hate and loathing: "If I ever had any racist feelings . . . I didn't know about it. But I can't imagine anyone in this world more prejudiced against the Negro than I am now. And two years ago, I swear to god I didn't feel like that" (37).

If Vincent is condemned as a heartless company man, the playwright seems to go even further in condemning Gloria for having allowed race to destroy her humanitarianism as well as her marriage. In act 2, in a monologue that is almost poetic, she implicitly agrees with Vince's judgment and accepts her share of the blame. She recalls walking down New York City streets and seeing some "really Harlemesque apartments" that aroused her sympathies for the people who lived in them. But when she realized the residents were not black, she lost interest. If she saw two boys playing in the street, one black and one white, she would automatically inspect the black boy for "some injury," hoping he'd be "lame or something." When she had worked as a school psychologist, however, the children had not been racial types but individuals whom she had tried to help indiscriminately. She recognizes that she has come to the point that she is no longer greatly concerned even about blacks, that she automatically rejects the poor regardless of color. "You crawled into your company and I crawled into a cocoon," she concludes (54).

At this point, Vince meets her halfway and admits that he should quit his job. She returns the gesture: "All I was saying, really, is that I've no room to talk about you. If I took stock of myself, I'd probably find I had no inventory" (54).

In act 1 Wilson seems to take a more critical view of Gloria as a black racist than he does of Vince as a designer of sterile, low-cost housing. This is redressed in act 2 by her long speech, which demonstrates some self-understanding on her part, while Vince is allowed no recognition of this sort, merely the simple admission of having gotten off the track, with a hint that he may try to change.

Before

As in many of Wilson's plays, there is in *The Gingham Dog* an evocation of an earlier time when things were different. In contrast with the present—the broken marriage set in a barren, white apartment—the past was the first year or so of the marriage when they had lived in a "hutch," a small apartment located on Sixth Avenue over the Waverly Theatre in Greenwhich Village. Vince grew a beard and played basketball across the street in a small park with a group of blacks. One of these friends, who had raised rabbits back in Georgia, named their apartment the "hutch" because "you can't imagine how cramped it got with eight or ten basketball players packed in there eating spaghetti" (24). This was the Golden Age of

their marriage: friends both black and white, basketball, food, love
in a small cramped bedroom. Vince had worked at designing store-
fronts then, but as Gloria says, "that was hardly what he was
looking for." After six months at another address, they had moved
to their present apartment, which seems little better than—in fact,
ironically to evoke—the kind of sterile living space Vince is designing as replacement for slums.

Upward mobility brought corresponding change, a diminution
in the quality of their relationship. The bed, which Gloria had
bought on their marriage, is a recurring symbol. Vince urges her
to keep it; at first she refuses, then agrees to keep it out of necessity.
Finally, it is a symbol of Vince's displacement when Gloria, dreading
to be alone, brings home a Spaniard, her "hot pepper," as Vince
calls him.

Conclusion

Although it may be of the 1960s, *The Gingham Dog* holds up
remarkably well. And although it may deal with political issues, it
goes far enough beyond them that it ceases, finally, to be merely a
political play while remaining a social one. The issues are political,
but the themes are universal and humanistic. In addition to the
major theme of a broken, interracial marriage, the play touches on
ambition, racial stereotypes, provinciality, southern "blinkers," and
obliquely, slum housing (similar in this respect to Shaw's *Widowers'
Houses*). The play is remarkable for its focus and economy. The two
minor characters, Robert and Barbara, are carefully motivated in
their few appearances, and the rest of the play concentrates on the
two principals. Unlike the majority of Wilson's plays of this period,
this work is entirely realistic in technique. There is no dramatic
artifice and no experimentation to break the dramatic illusion.

The Gingham Dog may remain one of Wilson's less popular plays
because it is strong and unpleasant and lacks a happy ending. But
it is a wise play, with trenchant, funny dialogue and well-observed
characters. It is a drama that, while it says something about America
in the 1960s, says more about marriage, the forces that divide, and
the humanity that cracks under the strain of contemporary life. It
is a very substantial achievement by a young playwright in a restless
and uncertain decade.

Chapter Seven
Lemon Sky

"Directly autobiographical" is the way Wilson describes *Lemon Sky*, first produced in 1970 at Buffalo and, a few weeks later, Off-Broadway. He also calls it his first "real play." He was only in his early twenties when he conceived the idea, and because he was dealing with painful events, he found it a difficult play to write: "I'd been trying to work on it for years and not getting anywhere, so I'd just put it aside and write something else."[1] *Lemon Sky* is a probing, personal statement, touching, funny, and painful, of a modern American Telemachus who, in a tranquil Eisenhower summer, finds his father, not in a midwestern Ithaca but in exotic California, only to fail in becoming a son to him. After opening at the Playhouse in New York, the play lasted only sixteen performances. When it was revived for a limited run Off-Broadway late in 1985, the *New York Times* described it as a "fine play . . . given exquisite new life."[2]

Plot: "How Can I Write about Dad?"

"I had the usual stepfather problems," Wilson says of his years in Ozark with his mother and her second husband. "Actually, I guess he was okay to me. . . . It's just that I wanted a father so *badly,* and here I both had one and I didn't have one." Sometime early in 1956, Wilson went to California to live with his father, whom he had seen only once in thirteen years. "We took an instant dislike to one another," he recalls, but he and his stepmother got along well, and, as in the play, he liked his two much younger stepbrothers.[3]

Lemon Sky is a *drama á clef* about this West Coast year, 1957, when Alan, the son, is seventeen. These scenes, however, are narrated and directed by a twenty-nine-year-old Alan, who in 1969, would have been only three years younger than Wilson. Act 1 covers approximately the son's arrival that spring morning and his first twenty-four hours in California. The shorter second act, covering a period of late spring and early summer, deals with Alan's settling-in for summer school at San Diego State College, in addition to full-time employment. Act 3 begins in late summer and charts the rapid disintegration of the father-son relationship as Doug, the father, reverses an earlier judgment and insists that Alan is nothing at all like him. This change is paralleled by the breakup of the "larger" family—Alan and the two seventeen-year-old wards of the state, Penny and Carol—who live with Doug and Ronnie and their two young sons, Jerry and Jack. Concluding in early autumn, *Lemon Sky* follows the seasonal cycle of life, growth, decline, and death.

The play's action is minimal: a son attempts to come to terms not only with a father he has hardly known since the age of five but also with a strange new landscape, new siblings and friends, and new society at work and school. *Lemon Sky* is a portrait, not so much painted as gradually revealed, of a father and husband with a far from perfect record who may be about to repeat old mistakes. At the same time, it is a faded photograph of seventeen-year-old Alan who is eager for a ready-made family but generally unshaped in other respects, a boy who will develop over the next dozen years into the fledgling playwright that Wilson himself was around 1959–60. It is the ironic detachment, humorous sensitivity, and objective honesty of this older narrator that gives the play particular poignance and dimension, not the dictatorial selfishness of Doug. Alan attempts to expiate any guilt he may have for his share of the fiasco and to exorcise it through dramatization. But he refuses exoneration, a gesture that augurs well for him as a person and for his ultimate forgiveness of his father.

The eternal, universal patterns of the search for a father, the longing for a lost son, the inability of two blood-related men to both love and forgive—all this is both content and theme in *Lemon Sky*. "You can't separate a kid from his father" recurs throughout the play like an epithetic formula from a folk epic. And concomitant is the universal need to belong: "I always wanted a big old family like this," Alan remarks; "it's just great."[4] With the need to belong goes the need for roots, a place: "I'm home today . . .," says Alan; "Oh, wow. And it is [home] now. Really is." (36). Finally, underlying these three thematic motifs—the need for father, for family, for home—is an atmosphere of marital discord, minor perhaps in *Lemon Sky* but very prominent in other works like *Gingham Dog* and *Serenading Louie*.

Alan: Teenager and Playwright

Wilson recalls that a favorite Ozark High School English teacher, Rex Bowers, who was also in charge of dramatics, "mercilessly cut" *The Glass Menagerie* down to a one-act play, so it could be entered in a play contest. "I was Tom, and it was a terrific experience. I just loved it."[5] Like *The Glass Menagerie, Lemon Sky* is a memory play in which the rememberer has become an artist who imposes his own order on events. Alan is Wilson's version of Tom. At twenty-nine, he draws upon the "magic" of theater to conjure up a younger, seventeen-year-old self around whom the action revolves.

Alan immediately confides to the audience, "I've been trying to tell this story, to get it down, for a long time." "I've had the title, I've had some of the scenes a dozen times, a dozen different ways" (7). His characters, however, like their real-life prototypes, behave badly for him. Moreover, he does not want to depict himself as the hero; indeed, he is not sure he *has* a hero. What comes through most clearly in Alan's opening monologue is the honesty of his intentions, his wish to portray what really happened in California by letting his memory speak, by letting the story "tell itself and *Mirror*, by what you couldn't say—what was really there" (8). This celebration of truth by invoking *Hamlet* ("to hold, as 'twere, the mirror up to nature") is Alan's finest quality.

As both narrator and character, Alan has several functions: he describes his own past and gives a brief background for the other characters; he is a bridge between the past and the present; and he provides a holistic view of the setting—the house, the topography, the climate, the weather, and California as the "edge of the continent." He also has a foreshadowing function: he speaks of having always wanted a big family but tells us that "it's not going to last." As narrator, he facetiously criticizes his own play-writing: "There'll be a scene," he promises the audience, anticipating their wish for a fuller explanation; "Those who are confused will say thank God, something to watch" (18). As director, he stages scenes—for example, his first meeting with Ronnie: "You are discovered," he tells her, "in a garden hat so the California sun doesn't burn you (10). He plays tricks with time when he reminds Carol that she has been dead for ten years. (She takes the opportunity to "thank the drear management for the magic of the theatre which enables me to be continually young and alive and beautiful" [42]). At the

end of act 3, Alan's last word is "Lights," usually a stage direction
but here also a reminder that he has finished his narrative of events
of a dozen years ago, and it is time to return to the present and
reality.

Doug: A Lost Father

Lemon Sky opens in darkness with barely defined characters on
stage—Wilson says "we should 'feel' they are there without actually
seeing them" (7). As Alan's opening monologue concludes, his father
begins to emerge from the darkness of a past relegated to the attic
of memory. As Doug begins to speak, the other characters answer
him from the stage twilight, and the scene finally blooms in the
brilliant sunlight of a California morning, the morning of Alan's
arrival.

At the end of the play, the reverse happens: Doug and Ronnie
are together at one side of the stage, and father and son are "very
far apart." As the stage darkens, Doug calls to Alan "as though
across time," repeating his desire to help the son he deserted. As
the lights dim, Alan is left alone in a spotlight, just as he was when
the play began, while voices tumble over each other in layered
dialogue, repeating lines from earlier scenes. When Alan calls
"Lights," the stage once again is brightly lighted. He walks off,
deserting the ghosts he has conjured up, as the stage returns to
darkness.

Perhaps Alan—and Wilson—are most effective in creating their
portrait of Douglas, for it is he who dominates the play. Before
Doug ever speaks, Alan tells us that he only lived with his father
for six months. "What do I know about him," he wonders. "If he's
nothing, I mean *But nothing!* Then the fact that he comes off the
short end of the stick shows something. From that you know that
there's *more* there" (8). He realizes that because of his emotional
reaction to Doug, there has to be more to him than he has seen,
and he does not want to be unfair.

Alan's first impression of Doug fulfills his dream of the father he
so long had desired: "A very distinguished looking man . . . so
handsome, . . . so good-looking, so young." Their embrace em-
barrasses Alan but pleases his father: *"Hugged me! Hugged me by God!"*
(8).

As Wilson makes clear, Doug is a romantic whose notion of

fatherhood is summed up in the recurring truism "you can't separate a kid from his father," an ironic reminder that he has seen Alan only once in the preceding twelve years. He must convince himself that the separation is not his fault: "I wanted you out here years ago," he tells his son, implying that Alan's mother is responsible, (9). He talks easily of getting Alan a car so he can work and attend college too, but it is clearly work that is uppermost in his mind. Carol points out that only Doug would still try to get in a half day at work on the first day in five years that he has seen his eldest son.

In act 2 we see a different side. Doug is critical of Alan for taking time off from work at the plant. He is disdainful of his college friends. They are "creepy creeps" who "look like they're made out of unbaked dough" (47). (Joan, Owen, Sasha, all characters in *The Sand Castle,* are mentioned in this scene.) Douglas has recently taken up photography, and his preoccupation with coaxing cheesecake models into and then half out of the same tacky red-white-and-blue bikinis at amateur photographer meetings has become a family joke among the three teenagers. He rarely takes photos of his family, however, and he destroys the one picture of his three sons taken at the beach the day after Alan's arrival.

Near the end of act 2, Doug asks Alan to contribute to his room and board. When his father turns authoritarian, Alan becomes distraught. In addition, Doug has attempted to seduce Carol, who is much too clever and worldly for him, and having failed there, has turned his attention to Penny (whose plainness is her hallmark), who is so upset that she refuses to stay in the house any longer. The picture of the handsome, loving father is completely shattered by the end of act 2.

Act 3 begins with the image of fire and is followed by Carol's account of her own fiery death the following year. The play's climax comes with Doug's vicious attack on Alan; he fears he may be seeing Penny's boyfriend, a man who Doug thinks is homosexual. When Doug orders Alan to leave, Alan blames him for the death of his sister who was stillborn thirteen years before. Doug strikes him, protesting that his son has no idea of "what that did to me," and orders him out of the house (65). While young Alan attempts to defend himself against his father's charges, it is clear that the older Alan realizes that he disappointed his father in not being the kind of son Doug wanted.

The other characters from Alan's past are all adequately drawn.

Ronnie, his stepmother, is understanding and sympathetic. His relationship with the two younger brothers, Jerry and Jack, is one of the nicest things in the play. Carol and Penny, both seventeen, are minor variations of the theme of neglected and abused children. Carol is tragically wise beyond her years and dies horribly in an auto accident, while plain Penny settles into a teacher's role.

Setting

Wilson gives special attention to every aspect of the stage setting, which in his description, recalls Willy Loman's house in *Death of a Salesman.* "More indicated than represented realistically," the house is defined by the "low sloping roofline against a broad expanse of sky." There are no walls, only "indicated division of rooms" (4). Characters sometimes move according to the layout of the house and at other times ignore "walls." If much of the action took place in Willy's mind in Arthur Miller's play, the action of *Lemon Sky* takes place entirely in Alan's memory.

Darkness is the boundary between forgetting and remembering, so the characters are conjured out of darkness at the beginning of the play and return into darkness at the end. The force and clarity of memory are suggested by the playwright's note that "as many scenes as possible are bathed in a bright cloudless sunlight (4). The sky is "never yellow," Wilson emphasizes, only the unnatural "lemon" of the title, and there is "no green in set or costume" (4).

Alan implies in his opening speech that he has had his title for a long time, but he never clearly explains it, saying only that it "had something to do" with California and the "nut fringe." Wilson probably colored his sky lemon to evoke a gaudy and altogether unnatural quality in the state and in the affected and artificial lifestyle of many who live there. "Lemon" suggests the garishness of neon signs, cheaply made Cinecolor movies, and bizarre billboards. Since California is a hyperbolic state in which real life aspires to be as large and unnatural as screen life, Alan feels it necessary to exaggerate the length of his stay there: two years "sounds more romantic," whereas "six months is like you didn't fit in" (7). It is too near the truth.

Wilson's California of the mid-1950s is characterized by mountains with exotic names, often ominously on fire; it is a place where the traffic is so heavy that people boast of it, a state of statistics that seem inflated even if they are not ("There's supposed to be four hundred new residents in California every day" [12]). It is a place where the Gold Rush is still on, Doug tells Alan enthusiastically. The climate is a "mess" briefly in March and April, and after that, no rain—and no green. ("The color green," says Carol, "does not occur in California naturally" [43]). Alan (like the playwright) has grown up in the Midwest, and greenless landscapes carry more than a hint of sterility.

Act 1 ends on a particularly ominous note: they all sit on the patio, smiling and tense, concentrating on the tremors of an earthquake, a natural phenomenon and a metaphoric harbinger of family discord. The mountain fires, which turn the sky red, quickly reduce the natural and manmade habitat to a "landscape that looked like the moon." Alan remembers that he "left Nebraska to come to the promised land because I had to" (58). But the promised land has proved unpromising; it is a state, mentally and geographically, of last resort, the ultimate point in the search for father and family. As Alan said earlier, "This is where I had to come to—right to the edge of the continent," which becomes a precipice in human relations when Doug delivers his "I call the shots" speech (54).

We leave Alan, six months after the events of the play, sleeping in a park in Chicago, back at least on his own geographical terrain. Since he represents Landford Wilson, we know it all somehow worked out, that the young man, who had characters, scenes, and even a title, was finally able to write his play—this play—and come to terms with the California past.

Conclusion

In structure, tone, and even themes, *Lemon Sky* owes something to works by the two giants, Miller and Williams, who dominated serious drama when Wilson was growing up. But Wilson weaves his own variations, and the play is highly engaging in its youthful vigor. Like much of Wilson's early work, it promises an original and refreshing voice in American drama.

Chapter Eight
One-Act Plays, 1967–1972
Untitled Play

Untitled Play, which Wilson finished in the spring of 1967, was written for the La Mama troop, and the characters were given the names of the actors and actresses who would play them. La Mama never produced the play, however, and early in 1968, it was done by the Judson Poets' Theater. Wilson now describes the play as an interesting failure. It has not been published.

Untitled Play is a curious amalgam of four quite dissimilar plot elements: the first involves Pierrot and Pirouette (Marie-Claire and Peter); the second, a group of actors who perform the "untitled" play that Pierrot and Pirouette (and the audience) watch; the third, a story of Michael's childhood, which he tells directly to the audience; and fourth, a play performed by four actors for the rest of their group and watched too by Pierrot and Pirouette.

On a bare stage, with no indication of time or place, Pierrot and Pirouette frame the other three plot elements but remain aloof from the action, although they sometimes comment on it. Peter carries onstage eight-inch, white cubes with which he builds a "tower." Mari-Claire spreads a large white scarf on the floor, which she reclaims at the end of the play, causing his tower to fall.

Michael introduces the "play" that his group will perform. It is "not so much untitled as ignoble," he tells the audience, "not so much play as games; but where Ignoble Games is totally obscure, Untitled Play has a————," and his voice trails off.[1] The group begins to "build" (in dialogue) a country with towns, cities, and countryside. A very long sequence of one-line speeches presents a cross section of national life in one verbal kaleidoscope.

After a country and society have been created, the builders realize that they are about to be attacked by another country. They invite the real audience to "stand with us" as they sing a rousing national anthem. The attack comes, and there is a battle.

In a sudden shift of mood, a postbattle entertainment, "rather

Pinter" in style, is quickly arranged. ("That's Culture," says Wilson.)[2] This play-within-a-play-within-a-play involves an aristocratic old lady and a sea captain. The old lady's son, Love, enters, followed by the captain's daughter, Dear. Love and Dear discover each other and fall into comically stylized copulation on the floor where they go unnoticed by their parents.

Michael stands in for Wilson. He is, the playwright says, a "real" character, unlike the others. In two long speeches, he recalls his family, his hometown on a river, and his home, a large white house with a wide lawn. He tells of a time—he was seven—when another boy beat him severely for no reason. He also tells the audience of childhood games he played on driveways and lawns, games that mirrored in their violence the reality of that beating: "We would build a town, a country, a civilization—spending just enough time on it to make it important to us and then blow it up."

The climax comes when all the group (except Mari-Claire and Peter) turn on a character named Victor, torment him, attack him, and tear his clothes off. He is left lying on the floor, completely naked and humiliated.

The characters of all four plot elements conclude the play on the same melancholy note: each group laments humanity's propensity for violence and its inclination to destroy what it has built. There is nothing noble in these games of men—"ignoble games"—hence, the rather strained pun of "untitled play." The theme of this short piece is "the evils of patriotism," Wilson says, and how, unleashed, they can lead to war by appealing to the aggression in everyone.[3]

Untitled Play is experimental in its attempt to blend four dissimilar plot elements. It projects a wide range of moods, moving as it does from the delicate tone of the Mari-Claire/Peter scenes to the pantomimed war and the savagery directed at Victor to the parody of Pinter. *Untitled Play* employs direct address, songs, balletic dance, blackouts, plays-within-plays, layered dialogue, parody, satire, symbolism, mime, and abrupt shifts in mood. It really does not work very well, and Wilson was right not to publish it.

Sa Hurt?

Sa Hurt?, an unpublished one-act play that Wilson wrote in 1968, is completely realistic in style and in no way experimental. This slice-of-life sketch of a husband and wife in prebreakfast conversation

is not one of Wilson's better short plays. Bud and Jenny Archer
have been happily married for over two years and have spent their
entire married life in the same small, cluttered apartment. In their
mid-twenties, both are actors whom Wilson describes as not greatly
talented, probably no more than adequate. On this Monday afternoon, they eat a very late breakfast while she reads a script.

Gradually, out of their random conversation, two problems emerge:
(1) he has not acted for a long time, and they have been living on
her modest wages as understudy; (2) she has not been feeling well
the preceding few weeks and is fearful she may be pregnant. If this
is true, she will have to give up her job, and Bud will have to find
some kind of work to support them. They both want children but
not yet, later—"when we have a decent apartment."[4]

The preceding month they had returned late from a party at
which she had become "smashed." He had helped her to bed and
made love to her without the precautions she normally took. But
he insists he had used a contraceptive. "She's so afraid she'll be a
mama," he teases her, and she replies, "Yes, and he's so afraid I
will—cause then his chips are down and he's got to get off his ass."
She speaks of seeing a doctor; he encourages her to do so, yet she
decides to put it off for a week. The play concludes with an affectionate dance, "both looking rather vacantly off over the other's
shoulder."

The play really does not take these two people very far. Jenny is
the better drawn character, although she is never more than moderately interesting. Bud's behavior is rather ambiguous. Clearly he
resents his inability to find work, and of course he dislikes living
on his wife's wages; but he does not seem inclined to do much about
it. Encouraging her to give up her modest job as understudy before
he has obtained work is very impractical. Has he told the truth
about using a contraceptive, or did he want to get her pregnant so
she would have to quit work, thus forcing himself to find employment? For that matter, it is not certain she *is* pregnant, so there is
a "what if" mood to the play that is never resolved. Their relationship is drawn with some subtlety, but it is never very engaging.

Sa Hurt? is a sketch of two rather ordinary people who have
drifted into marital and professional problems. We may wonder
briefly what will become of them, even if Jenny is not pregnant,
but we will not wonder long or care deeply. The title of the play,
which may be translated as "Does it hurt?", is an affectionate ques-

tion couched in the accents of childhood. Yes, Jenny hurts, and although Bud may be loving and sympathetic, he may also be responsible for hurting her. This is a play about the pressures on young marrieds—and young actors—that foreshadow pain as they build a life together.

Stoop

Although *Stoop* was written for television and first presented as a segment of *Foul!* on "New York Television Theater" in 1969, it would work just as well on stage. It is very short, perhaps eight to ten minutes, and very carefully constructed. It is realistic in style but slightly experimental in mood, for it pays a very modest homage to the absurdist plays of the 1950s and 1960s.

Three women (one of whom never speaks), all between fifty and sixty, sit on the stoop of a run-down brownstone dwelling. Their conversation is desultory; most of their lines are "spoken philosophically." The theme involves, first, physical deterioration on a personal level: the First Woman is having trouble with her back, while the Second Woman has trouble with her kidneys. (She "wets" when she laughs; i.e., she is, ironically, affected only when she is happy.)

The theme also works on another level: there has been a plague or epidemic, and dead bodies are placed on the sidewalks to be picked up. "They collected them late today," comments the First Woman. "They're getting so they don't pick up till nearly noon," replies the Second Woman; "bodies laying all over the streets— now, that's not healthy."[5] The plague has forced them to drink "canned water," and the radio stations have been off the air. The two also discuss a strange smell that comes neither from a manufacturing plant nor the river. It is, they decide, the odor of dead bodies burning.

The play achieves its effect by contrasting the casual attitude of the three women with the dimensions of a major catastrophe. Their everyday exchange of symptoms and family gossip is no less— possibly more—important than the deaths of hundreds around them. Because of this, the tone of the play invites comparison with a work like Shirley Jackson's short story "The Lottery."

The three women are nevertheless affected by what has happened, although they are beyond excitement. To show this, the playwright appeals to the four senses. In the first speech of the play, the First Woman complains that when she went to the doctor for an examination of her back, he "didn't once touch me. . . . I told him, I can't bend over. I can't pick up. He tells me stoop" (65). At the end of the play, she returns to her problem: "I said I can't pick up," she repeats. "He says what's to pick up? Now, what kind of attitude is that? Don't pick up" (68).

Of course, the dramatist is playing on the word "stoop"; it is both setting and a common body movement. But the doctor had said there was nothing to stoop for—the action has no point. All this, coupled with talk of the plague (only referred to as "it"), evokes a Beckettean mood of finality.

The sense of smell is captured when they speak of smoke from the burning bodies; of taste, when they speak of fruit having little flavor. And throughout the play, a child practices "My Old Kentucky Home" on a piano somewhere in the neighborhood. At the end of the play, after many mistakes and pauses, the unknown player makes it through the first line of the song without error, causing all three women to look offstage with surprise. The sentimental old Stephen Foster ballad comments ironically on the ugly, moribund cityscape these women face from their front stoop: both time and place are too ugly for sentiment.

The shadow of Samuel Beckett falls briefly across this little television playlet, just as the smell of the unidentified plague taints the view from Wilson's American front porch, transformed here into the steps of a metropolitan brownstone. *Stoop* is a slight but honorable work.

Victory on Mrs. Dandywine's Island

"What is a positive play?" Wilson asked the director, David Marlin-Jones. "Tell me something that you can examine and examine in depth that comes out positive." Wilson and Marlin-Jones were in Washington, D.C., in the spring of 1970 for the premiere of *Serenading Louie,* and the playwright was disturbed by the negative effect the play was having on theatergoers, some of whom were visibly upset by his bleak vision of marriage and the Good Life in the upper middle classes of the late 1960s. His director was no help: "As soon as I think of something, you'll be the first to know."[6]

To try to answer his own question, the playwright set himself a

simple exercise: to write a short piece in which good triumphs over
evil. That was the only reason he wrote *Victory on Mrs. Dandywine's
Island.* It was not meant for publication or production. But a pub-
lisher happened to see it and wanted to include it in a collection of
short plays, so it got into print. It should never have been published,
Wilson feels now, for as an experiment it does not work.

Mrs. Dandywine is set in a cottage living room on an island, which
is a salt flat and therefore sterile ground. The living room belongs
to Mrs. Dandywine, a stout, over-fifty, somewhat aristocratic lady,
who is cared for by a companion, Miss Companion, also over fifty
and "both excitable and impressionable."[7] They are visited by Mr.
Orfington, a sedate, middle-aged gentleman. There is also a Gardener whose dialogue is a series of "mum, mum, mum"s and an
enemy-neighbor, Miss Liveforever.

There is not much action for most of this short play. A very loud
knocking on the floor of the living room ("our mysterious circum-
stance") occurs several times; this is followed by a dramatic confrontation between the Gardener and Miss Liveforever, who threatens
Mrs. Dandywine and her employee ("I'll flood your yard with horse
piss"), blaming them for some unexplained development (71).

After these two reach a standoff, Miss Companion is sent outside
to investigate whatever has happened. She returns to report that
"the ground is cracked and something appears to be pushing up,"
something green that seems to be a bulb (73). After more thunder
and lightning, a badly scorched Miss Liveforever (her house has just
burned to the ground) reappears to announce defiantly that she will
continue her struggle against Mrs. Dandywine and the Gardener.
Mr. Orfington, having gone outside to check, reports that the bulb
has shoots; shortly after, Miss Companion announces that it is a
hyacinth and that it is blooming. Mr. Orfington leaves, as Mrs.
Dandywine languorously threads her way through her "history"—
her favorite subject—recalling that "through will I overcame. I
don't remember what it was I overcame. I remember only a sense
of victory which has remained with me ever since" (78).

Wilson agrees that this little "doodle" might be labeled a "morality play," since, as in that late medieval form of drama, some of
its characters are abstractions of virtue and vice. His original intention was to work with "the very simplest elements," and so "I
didn't try to create character depth." Miss Liveforever is the "devil's
angel," a force of Evil, while the Gardener is her opposite, the angel

of Good, who encourages life and growth in the sterile soil of the island, which is a metaphor for Earth. The bulb is the force of Good; the knocking under the floor and the thunder are the clashes of Good and Evil. The other three characters, Wilson says, are "just stupid little mortals who have no idea of what's going on": a woman who is totally absorbed in herself, a woman who tries to get things done, and a man who is baffled by everything.[8]

Although neither characters nor setting is identifiably English or American, we are told that the play "should be treated in the exaggerated high style associated with an English Comedy of manners" (65). It is therefore tempting to see Mrs. Dandywine as a minor variant of Oscar Wilde's Lady Bracknell (*The Importance of Being Earnest*), but Wilson will only say she is "not unlike" that character although not deliberately patterned on her.

Mrs. Dandywine is a curious blend of comedy of manners and morality play, with a dash of allegory. Years after it was written, Wilson saw it in a workshop production and pronounced it "abominable" and "awful." Still, these characters, so unlike most Wilson has created, are interesting within the narrow range he gives them, especially Mrs. Dandywine, Miss Companion, and Mr. Orfington. Some of the latter's innocently blunt pronouncements recall the disarming frankness of Wilde's "earnest" Victorians. Although unsuccessful as a play, *Mrs. Dandywine* is a perfectly honorable experiment.

Sextet (Yes)

Sextet (Yes) is an experimental "play for voices" that Wilson wrote in 1970 for the Center Theatre Group of Los Angeles. It is "scored" for six people who, in varying degrees, have sex on their minds: three middle-aged men and three women, two of whom are middle-aged, while one is in her twenties. They are seated on chairs randomly on a bare stage. At first, the six figures are "backlit," but the lighting grows during the play and fades near the end, perhaps suggesting a cycle such as a day or a lifetime. They speak in voices "rather removed, not too involved."[9]

"Yes" recurs throughout the play like a refrain, suggesting "quiet confirmation." It may indicate acceptance of fate and fact, or it might merely imply acquiescence with a husband, wife, or lover. All speakers use the past tense, which, in their impassive, unemotional reading of the lines, suggests that they are in a state beyond—or somehow out of—life, a point beyond passion, love, and other emotions. They are never aware of an audience, nor do they ever speak to each other. They are Melvillian isolatoes.

Perhaps *Sextet (Yes)* is best seen as a young playwright's miniversion of Arthur Schnitzler's *La Ronde,* set, one may guess, in New York City in the 1960s. Bert (whose wife is not one of the six characters), is having an affair with Betsy, who is married to Bill, who is having a platonic affair with Brenda, the youngest of the group and the only one not married. Bill's brother, Bob, is married to Belle (a widow). The dialogue of these people is, in essence, six monologues that have been broken into short speeches and then orchestrated, very skillfully, into a brief vignette. The result tells a great deal about all six and their society.

The three men are commuters, perhaps living in Connecticut or Long Island. Brenda lives in New York City; Belle still commutes to the city as she did during her first marriage; Betsy awaits both lover and husband at her home in the suburbs. Most of these six people are acquainted with the other five. Each character slowly creates a social environment of things and people important to that character.

Bill, who begins and ends the play, recalls that he married Betsy after proposing to "about eight girls." He had a routine of sex once a month with her, but his relationship with Brenda came to mean more to him than his family or his job: "It was a new life! It was like living again" (76). While he never had sex with Brenda, in the last speech of the play he recounts a very erotic dream in which they made love deep in a wood and bedded on "soft chartreuse grass" (79).

Brenda, however, has almost forgotten Bill: "Smallish eyes, almost no lashes, yes," she recalls vaguely (73). "He used to kiss me but it was as a father" (75). She remembers going to galleries and concerts with him, but is uncertain whether it was he or another man who had taken her to eat at all those "ethnic places that only locals frequented" (73). Brenda alone never speaks of marriage.

Bert's speeches are the most erotic as he describes his affair with Betsy, Bill's wife. He returned earlier than Bill from his job in the city, and "a couple of times a week Betsy and I went at it" (77). Betsy remembers Bert's first advance to her, which ended in a handshake, "and we knew what it meant. What it signalled." She compares the way Bert made love to her with her husband's technique. But she does not complain of Bill, who was "an excellent provider" and "good with the kids" (78).

Bob and his brother (Bill) had grown up in the West and Midwest where they had worked with horses, and these recollections of their youth figure prominently in Bob's thinking. He is also preoccupied with his marriage at middle-age, his first, to Belle. He consoles himself that he was easy to get along with, even thugh he could not give her expensive things, as her first husband had. Bob occasionally sings bits of an old cowboy ballad ("Bang the Drum Slowly"), which appropriately is a lament for the dead.

Sextet (Yes), slight though it is, works very well. In tone and setting, it is somewhat expressionistic. It may also simply be another modest homage to the absurdists. If it is Wilson's version of a state somehow beyond life, there is never any sense of punishment or regret. It is, in any case, a skillful exercise by a still young author who was writing of adultery in *Serenading Louie* in these same years, a period when the playwright was both social observer and experimenter.

Ikke, Ikke, Nye, Nye, Nye

After a first production in New Haven at the Yale Cabaret, *Ikke, Ikke, Nye, Nye, Nye* became a part of a bill of short works (including *The Family Continues*) given by the Circle Repertory Company in May 1972. It is Wilson's attempt at farce. It is atypical of his work in general and not especially important, but it is funny enough to justify his experiment.

Graham, a thirty-five-year-old "bewildered child," is the mail boy for the New York firm of Skidney, Scheindecker, Hornblower and Bicks. He is also the son of a company boss who has promised to make him a vice-president if he does well in the mailroom. He and Edith, a telephone operator for the firm, have returned to her apartment after an evening at the theater. Edith, also about thirty-five, flatters him, makes him drinks, and generally tries to "vamp" him. Graham seems incredibly proper and naive at first ("Actually I've never been in anyone's apartment before. . . . Not physically at least").[10] But when Edith leaves to make drinks in the kitchen, he grabs the telephone, dials, and "with desperate urgency" breathes heavily five times into it when someone answers.

Ikke, Ikke is a short farce about a telephone fetishist. Graham,

who carries a pocket full of dimes, is exceedingly prim while fe-
rociously searching out any telephone. Most of the humor depends
on his attempts to make obscene calls while Edith is out of the
room on some errand. When she returns, he slams down the receiver,
sits on the phone or hides it behind the daybed, and generally makes
it the object of visual, physical comedy. Having become slightly
drunk, he substitutes a half-full martini glass for the telephone,
and after shouting "hello," breathes heavily into it three times. The
martini stains on his trousers suggest the orgasmic nature of his
agitation.

While he is supposedly in the bathroom cleaning up, Edith receives an obscene call. The caller is Graham who is talking from
the telephone in her bedroom. He has finally found a way of communicating with her. Edith, for her part, is thrilled by her unknown
caller. His attempts to elicit a description of her anatomy arouse
mock indignation, pretended shock, and genuine fascination. We
know what he is saying to her from his earlier calls ("How big are
your—hello?" [56]), and she is pleased to provide shocked, im-
aginative answers ("large, milky white pendant cantaloupes" [60]).
After the conversation has reduced her to orgasmic exhaustion ("Smut.
Smut. Oh, smut" [60]), Graham returns from the bedroom, his old
proper self again. As he prepares to leave, Edith is left moaning
weakly, "Smut."

The title of the play (it rhymes with "picky") was a phrase Wilson
heard children's nannies use to their young charges in Copenhagen.
He does not know exactly what it meant, but to him it means
"nasty, nasty, no, no, no."[11] When Graham was a child, his father
had hired a French girl named Monique as his companion, but she
spoke only French and had subsequently run off with her employer.
Wilson meant to transform French Monique into a Danish au-pair
girl who might naturally have used the phrase to reprimand Graham
(although he never meant it to be spoken in the play). Somehow,
the change from the French name to a Danish name was never made,
so linguistically the title makes no sense, as Wilson admits. He has
been content to leave it that way and enjoy the comic incongruity
of the Danish phrase as the title of a play that has nothing to do
with Denmark.[12]

Actually Edith and Graham are two of Wilson's urban misfits
who owe something to the couple in the very early lost play, *So
Long at the Fair*. Their farcical loveplay almost obscures the fact that

they are two lonely, desperate people for whom the telephone is
"the only way either one . . . is going to have any sort of experience
whatsoever. They've had an absolutely wonderful—a very successful
date as far as I'm concerned," Wilson says.[13] Despite the sadness
underneath, *Ikke, Ikke* could be highly entertaining if properly performed, and it reveals the author's flair in territory he does not
normally explore.

The Family Continues

Subtitled "A Round," *The Family Continues* is the second of two
short pieces Wilson wrote for the Circle Repertory Company in
1972. His note on the play explains that it "should be considered
a game, an exercise in swift characterization and ensemble co-op-
eration."[14] Stage directions are minimal to allow the director and
players to work "unfettered." No furniture or props are required.
The dialogue is to flow continuously and overlap. It is not necessary
that all the words he heard, for whole sections are repeated. Wilson
emphasizes that the play is to be "done simply and with a sense of
joy in creation" (30). The director should "try anything" that will
illustrate the life of his main character. The total effect of the piece
is to be emphasized over any part of it.

The Family Continues evokes Shakespeare's "Seven Ages of Man"
speech in *As You Like It,* for this little "round" is Wilson's "Ten
Phases of Man" play. Presided over by a Narrator who announces
each "phrase," eight actors playing twenty-six characters dramatize
the life of a man, Steve, from birth to death. Included is the birth
of a son, Steve, Jr. Some "phases" encompass quite a lot; for example,
Phase One: "Getting born, learning to walk, learning to talk, the
family, meeting a playmate, going to grandma's"(33). Between
Phases One and Ten, Steve goes through many of the stereotypical
stages of maturation as well as some that are not. For example, by
the end of Phase Three, Steve has been responsible for the deaths
of two people and has been dishonorably discharged from military
service. After working in a gas station where he meets the Girl
(whom he marries), Steve himself becomes manager of the station,
after which Steve, Jr., becomes the focus of attention as he repeats
his father's scenes.

Phase Nine ("Old age and senility") comes on Steve so quickly
that he protests vehemently: "I don't buy your Phase nine. And I

don't buy your Phase one through eight" (46). In a slightly deranged state, Steve is confronted by his past when he sees the Kid, an eight-year-old he killed ("You ran right out in front of me" [48]) when he was younger. When Phase Ten ("Passing away") is announced, he is "overcome, stunned, scared, brave" (48). As the lights fade, he continues to protest and cajole in the often vulgar parlance he has used throughout.

The effectiveness of *The Family Continues* lies in the fact that in only a few minutes and on a bare stage, the actors are able to convey the pathos of a man's amazement at the fleeting nature of his life and the brevity of his existence on earth. Although most of Steve's (and Steve, Jr.'s) experiences are representative of those of a type of young male who came to maturity in the last thirty years, some are not. In fact, Steve and his son have attributes like those of Wilson's "outsiders" in the plays of the 1960s, for they are abusive, violent, and vulgar. The "joy in creation" the playwright calls for in dramatizing the life cycles of these two seems at odds with the type of people they are.

This is not to deny the vitality and exuberance the playwright brings to his own act of creation, for despite the ugly side of the two main characters, the piece rings with energy and verve. That Wilson was attracted to and influenced by the work of Thornton Wilder in these early years has been mentioned. *The Family Continues,* in particular, is an example of that influence in its evocation of Wilder's short play *The Long Christmas Dinner,* as well as *The Skin of Our Teeth.* It also seems likely that a theater piece like Richard Schechner's *Dionysus in 69* and the work of the Living Theater, so popular in the late 1960s, left their mark on this little "round." *The Family Continues* is minor Wilson, but it shows the playwright responding to his elders as well as to his peers, leaving little doubt that his energy and imagination would be channeled into more substantial work.

Chapter Nine
Serenading Louie

Wilson remembers sitting in the lobby of a Washington, D.C., theater in 1970 where *Serenading Louie* (in the initial and unpublished version) was premiering: "About eight people came out into the lobby to take tranquilizers. We really shook them up. And that had not been my intention at all—to wreck someone's evening."[1] *Louie* is indeed a very disturbing play and may well be Wilson's most pessimistic view of humanity's chances for happiness. It has a Strindbergian darkness of tone, although without the Swede's bitter misogyny, and there is no light at the end of the tunnel for the playwright's quartet of 1960s overachievers. Perhaps because violence seems quite alien to both characters and setting, an upper-class living room in an affluent Chicago suburb, the brutal murders at the end are particularly shocking.

After the production by the Washington Theater Club, the playwright revised the play for its May 1976 production by the Circle Repertory Company in New York City. This is generally recognized as the official premiere, since it was this version that was published. After further revisions, *Louie* was revived in February 1984, at the Public Theater in New York, where it was respectfully reviewed ("sensitive, serious, honest, funny, unsatisfying, and tremendously worthy") but still found to be "imperfect—very, very imperfect."[2]

The revisions Wilson undertook for this third production were fairly minor: the first two scenes of act 1 were transposed; most of the lines directed to the audience (and there were many in the first published version) were now directed to other characters; lines were moved around within scenes, and some new lines were added here and there; minor references were changed to bring the play up to date. Wilson himself finds the play "very unsuccessful. It's some of the best writing I've done and the worst play."[3]

Plot

In the late 1960s, two couples in an affluent Chicago suburb reflect longingly on a seemingly golden past, even as they presently enjoy social and professional success. One couple, Carl and Mary (parents of young Ellen, never seen), lead such busy lives that they rarely have time for meaningful talk. Mary is having an affair with her husband's accountant, and Carl has been so successful that his friend Alex kids him about being "the youngest dead millionaire I know."[4]

Alex and Gabby seem, on the surface, very much like Carl and Mary. A successful lawyer, Alex has just been offered the opportunity for a political career in Washington. Gabby loves her husband and is not very concerned about being followed recently by an elderly man. Yet, as Alex confesses to Carl, he loves his wife "less and less" and has, in fact, developed a platonic attachment for a teenager whose vitality stirs in him dreams of hope and renewal.

Shortly after Halloween, the four spend a seemingly happy evening together, reminiscing about college days. Not long after, Carl, who has known of his wife's affair but who has done nothing, suddenly calls her accountant-lover and asks him "how about knocking it off with my wife" (55). But Mary refuses to end the affair. The elderly man following Gabby turns out to be the father of Debbie, the girl with whom Alex is infatuated. Gabby's confrontation with Alex portends a permanent break in their relationship. At the end of the play, Carl kills both his wife and daughter before committing suicide.

Carl: "Nothing Is an Event Anymore"

Since Carl is the most expressive of the four characters, his tragedy touches us most deeply. He can look back on a past that seems the very essence of growing up in Middle America. Recalling with affection the years he attended Sunday School, he laments that "everything was an Event then." Now "we don't have those anymore. Why is that? What's happened?" (19). Once the point of life was to be happy; now "life is a ballbreaker" (23).

His lament is more than merely personal; it is a tirade against the general disintegration of society. "Building" and "developing" used to be positive terms, not coupled, as they now are, with incessant striving for success. "I didn't know you had to get ahead," Carl tells Alex; "I thought you could just lope along." Business now amounts to "profiteering and pick-pocketing each other." Life is a "shell game," and "nobody's content with it" (23).

Even when Alex tells his friend what he already knows, that Mary is having an affair, Carl seems past the point of concern: "I see it like I see everything else—like I'm up in the air and it's down on the ground happening to someone else. It doesn't affect me." After nine years of marriage, Carl accepts Mary's infidelity as "no big deal" and insists "I can't get involved with anything" (29). Yet, after all this, he concludes the scene at a pitch not reached anywhere else in the play when he rages against Mary: "WHAT'S SHE TRYING TO DO? I DON'T KNOW WHAT TO SAY. I DON'T KNOW HOW TO FEEL, ALEX. . . . I WANT IT BACK—LIKE IT WAS. IT WAS GOOD THEN. IT WAS GOOD THEN, GODDAMNIT" (33).

This is the heart of the matter: youth was bright with expectations that life, even a life blessed with success, has not fulfilled. The American Dream has turned into a personal nightmare, even as it has come true. The strength of the play is the shock of recognition it elicits from an audience, attesting to the fact that the malaise is a common reaction.

Carl, once a very religious person, still prays regularly. He also believes in an apocalypse: "When the sky suddenly splits wide open one day and angels sing—you look up and say—thank God, I kept up my praying" (47). Yet, religion has given him no answers, and foreshadowing the end of the play, he warns that "it's all got to break."

In his last scene with Mary, he explains that even though he was a college football star and has had a successful career in business, none of it means anything except in terms of her love: "Nothing was of value if I couldn't lay it at a woman's feet some day as a sacrifice, a pledge!" He begs her to "tell me we can have it back the way it was" (61). She refuses. In his last conversation over the telephone with Alex, Carl is almost incoherent as he tries to reassure his friend that everything has been patched up. It is, in fact, his farewell to his best buddy, as Alex realizes too late to do anything.

Carl should have been in the "best years" of his life; yet these years proved to be a time of doubting and questioning. *Serenading Louie* is not a play with answers but one that asks questions about contemporary America: Why does the present fail to live up to the promises of the past? Why does the fruit of success seem to rot? Why does love die when there is every reason for it to thrive? Why does prayer no longer nourish the spirit? Why are we so ineffectual in helping ourselves and succoring those close to us? Why is getting what we want worse than not getting it? Wilson offers no answers, nor does he offer action in a play of inaction until the end when Carl overcomes his inertia and kills the wife and daughter he loves.

Alex: "Everywhere I look It's Falling Apart"

Although Alex's situation is not so complicated as Carl's, nor so tragic, the future seems to hold as little for him as it does for his friend. Gabby complains he sleeps all the time he is at home; she wonders if "there isn't someone else" (13). He denies it, but the fact that he lies to her about something so important says much about him. His lack of enthusiasm for a move to Washington is not clear until he admits his relationship with the teenage Debbie. For him, too, things are "falling apart."

Early symptoms of disintegration are a symbolic toothache and the fact that a beautiful old fountain pen, which had been his grandfather's, had leaked all over him in the middle of a court trial. "I keep feeling my real life will begin any day now," he tells Carl. "This can't be it. This is just temporary. A dry run" (21).

The disintegration of his relationship with Gabby is probably the most important factor in his unhappiness. When they go out with Carl and Mary, she is fine; he is in love with her and desires her. But when they come home, she is a different person. She becomes very seductive, and her "kisses all turn to tongue." Her attempts at lovemaking make him feel like a "temporary eunuch." "I'd just like to be reassured that I wasn't the world's only man who felt cut, gelded—after sleeping with his own wife. Ravaged. . . . I'd like just once . . . to ravage her!" (32). When Carl suggests he no longer loves Gabby, he answers that "you don't love someone all the time. You love them for moments" (28). And the moments of love, he realizes, are becoming fewer.

If Alex and Gabby are unable to agree on making love or conversation, they are also in disagreement concerning the younger generation. Gabby complains that student crowds make her feel nervous and threatened. Alex defends them, saying he would give anything to be seventeen again. Later, when he confesses to Carl that he may be in love with a teenager, he explains that he is amazed by what she knows, "things I don't even know yet" (53). He is afflicted with an early attack of "the seven-year-itch," which has less to do with sex than with fear of aging and a desire to reenact the ceremonies of youth.

Neither for major nor minor problems are there answers. Curiously, the one solution that comes to Alex like a nightmare is the solution to which Carl finally resorts. Alex imagines "that horrible moment when I feel I, myself, just might, one of these deranged and silvery mornings, become the monster you read about who slays his family and himself or fifteen strangers" (57).

When Gabby confronts her husband with his infidelity, Alex explains that he has "an image" of an ideal girl, not anyone specific, not Debbie and not Gabby. He realizes this image has caused him to resist "anything that strengthened our marriage—any real commitment." He offers to surrender this dream of an idealized lover in order to start over in Washington with Gabby. They should look outside themselves, he says, and "try to help . . . people who need us" (61). But Gabby refuses; his dream and his commitment are not for her. At this point, Alex answers Carl's final telephone call and rushes off to his friend's apartment to find the carnage he himself had imagined in a wild moment of his own agonies.

Alex and Gabby have evolved into a star-crossed, middle-aged married couple whose lives do not run on parallel courses. A seemingly happy married man, he realizes he no longer loves his wife and instead identifies with the younger generation through whom he tries to live vicariously. Willing to draw back and accept what he thought he had, he finds he cannot even retain that. He is almost as great a loser as Carl.

Mary and Gabby

Wilson's two female characters, while quite as believable as Carl and Alex, are not so fully fleshed out. Mary's is the simpler of the two roles, for she is principally the cause of Carl's collapse. She had been his college sweetheart, a homecoming beauty queen with whom he had lived before they were married. In one of the best lines in the play she confesses of Carl that "I don't actually think . . . that I loved him then. But I love him then now" (41). As one reviewer commented, "Translated, that means she didn't love him then and loves him even less now. It sounds innocent, conciliatory, and is devastating."[5]

We never hear very much from Mary of her love affair. Gabby tells Alex that Mary and the accountant were "apparently" in love, but Mary suggests to Carl that she saw the man "just because I got off on it" (56). She complains that what Carl feels for her "isn't love, it's self-sacrifice" (60). When he begs her to reassure him they can be happy once again, she refuses, saying, "I couldn't do that" (61). Far from experiencing love and its loss, she seems to have had nine years of marriage to a man of whom she was only fond. That, perhaps, is the scope of her tragedy.

Like Mary, Gabby is also revealed more in her husband's lines than in her own; still, she is a more fully developed character than her friend. Her life without her husband's affection is incomplete, for she still loves him. Her sense of fragmentation is reflected in her unfinished sentences and tentative thoughts. Alex describes her as someone who will go along with anything. She is not "the revolutionary type"; all she wants is home, children, and love. "I don't want to help anyone," she says, insisting she would "never be able to convince myself I wasn't helping someone to make myself feel noble, and I'd feel better making myself feel noble honestly" (62). Although she is the most normal of the four, she is unable (or unwilling) to change with changing societal attitudes. She is unhappy because things do not remain the same even as she herself does.

Dramatic Techniques

Wilson commented in an interview that *Serenading Louie* was one of his last plays to have "that flashy technique" characteristic of some of his early work, meaning that technique often overshadowed characterization.[6] What is "flashy" about *Louie* is primarily his manipulation of setting. A single living room set serves both couples. In act 1, a scene shift from one household to another is clearly delineated by blackouts. Act 2, however, has a number of scenes, some of them very short, and the blackouts are omitted, thus giving the act a very fluid structure. Readers, as distinguished from viewers, may occasionally be somewhat puzzled as to just where one scene leaves off and another begins.

The time of the action is late October and early November. By act 2, Halloween has just passed. Wilson's quartet of characters is haunted by happier spirits from the past but mostly by ghosts of unfulfilled lives. A decorative touch in the setting is a shadow puppet on the wall, perhaps hinting that the characters are manipulated by some external force. A reminder of the Halloween season is the plastic mask of a bull that Carl had worn when he made the trick-or-treat rounds of the neighborhood with Ellen, who had worn a calf's mask. Mary reminds Carl that she was born under the sign of Taurus, the bull. That the bull and calf are both animals of sacrifice in primitive rites subtly foreshadows the violence at the end of the play.

Perhaps the most poetic image is the leaf, here symbolic of autumn and death. In act 1, Gabby remembers that as a first grader on her way to school, she had picked up a bright red leaf covered with thick frost to bring to her teacher. She does not have to say that the frost on the leaf melted or that the leaf turned brown. It is a beautiful image of transience. Alex expresses his frustration in a comment about the men on his street who seem to spend their lives burning leaves, a metaphor for "killing time."

Finally, there is the title. All four characters are college graduates—three alumnae of Northwestern University and Gabby of Stevens College (in Columbia, Missouri)—but none attended Yale with which the famous "Whiffenpoof Song" is associated. They sing it nostalgically and somewhat drunkenly, as it is often sung, in the only happy scene of the play. The sentimentality of the song sorts well with their view of the past, for they are the "lost sheep" they sing about. (Carl had quoted earlier in the play a part of Psalm 23 in which sheep are metaphors for lost souls.) If "The Whiffenpoof Song" is a drinking song, drowning in a toast the troubles of generations of underclassmen, then in this play, to "serenade Louie" is to lament the unhappiness that time has brought to these four collegians of the Eisenhower years and to many of their generation. This scene concludes with the singing of the Christmas carol "God Rest Ye Merry, Gentlemen," wonderfully ironic here and pathetic too in its promise of salvation, holiday joy, and family love.

Themes: "The Way We Were"

Certainly *Serenading Louie* is one of Wilson's most explicit treatments of the theme of marital discord and adultery. It is also a play about the death of love with a backward look at love's beginnings. The past haunts the present in the form of happiness recalled. From Alex's point of view, the issues in *Louie* are time and change, hope for the future, and the desire to help even when one needs help. For Gabby, it is a question of unfulfilled love. For Mary, the issues are marrying for affection instead of love and the effects of infidelity. For Carl, they are the tragedy of love's failure and life's inability to compensate for it.

If *Serenading Louie* is wise in questions it contemplates, it is incomplete in its failure to suggest answers. As Wilson acknowledges, pessimism is the easy way. It is gratifying that he has subsequently taken the more difficult course of depicting characters who courageously seek and find answers.

Chapter 10
One-Act Plays of the 1970s
The Great Nebula in Orion

While Wilson was still working on *Serenading Louie,* he received a letter from the Stables Theatre Club in Manchester, England, explaining that its members had been doing a workshop production of *Ludlow Fair* and wished to move it, with a companion piece, into their main theater. They wondered if he had something suitable to go with it, obviously a piece for the same two actresses. The playwright was in a receptive mood; he already had, he says, "an Agnes shape and a Rachel shape," that is, two physical types—silhouettes—that he could fill in with very different characters.

The Manchester request had also found him "deep in college lore," as a result of his work on *Louie.* At this point, he remembered a short story he had written years ago in Chicago with the curious title "Fuzz on Orion's Sword." The story (with overtones of *The Bottle Harp*) involved a young woman from Boston who had come to visit her brother in New York. "Carrie's story was essentially already written in that short story," Wilson says. He then invented Louise, brought the two women together as old college friends, and set up the interplay between them. [1]

He had originally intended to call the new play *Bergdorf's to the Moon,* but as he worked on it, he became involved with the astronomical imagery and found his title there. He sent off a "terribly typed draft" to Manchester, but because of a postal strike in England, he heard nothing for six months. Finally a packet of reviews arrived, telling him the play had been well received. The American premiere was given by the Circle Repertory Company in 1972, where it was part of a triple bill.

Wilson likes *The Great Nebula in Orion* very much, and although it is contemporary with and even earlier than some of the one-act plays discussed previously, he does not feel it belongs in that group. For one thing, it is a better, more important play; for another, it is infused with the same collegiate spirit as *Serenading Louie,* so he tends to see the shorter work as an epilogue to the longer. Certainly *Great Nebula* is Wilson's best short play of the 1970s and one of his very best.

Two college friends, Carrie and Louise, meet by chance for the first time in seven years as they shop at Bergdorf Goodman's on Fifth Avenue. Although they had been quite close when they attended Bryn Mawr in the 1950s, they have now settled for exchanging Christmas cards. As they enter Louise's apartment on the Upper West Side of Manhattan, the old relationship begins to revive. What follows is a series of revelations that strip both women emotionally bare, showing that the glamorous exterior of success has little relation to the loneliness underneath, for just as Carrie is not the happily married young Boston matron she seems, neither is Louise the carefree, sophisticated star of the New York fashion world.

At thirty-four, Louise is a year older than Carrie and a top fashion designer, the youngest ever to win a major award. She is lonely and, therefore, genuinely pleased to see her old friend, whom she envies for her seemingly ideal family. But when Carrie casually opens the door to Louise's bedroom, she sees a photograph of a former classmate, Phyllis, who is, in fact, Louise's former lover. Together Louise and Phyllis had furnished the apartment, but Phyllis had left six years before, and Louise had stayed on alone. Carrie is a little shaken at her discovery of their liaison, for they had just been discussing the other woman, and Louise had pretended ignorance of her.

Carrie, at thirty-three, has a wealthy husband and two beautiful children, a house in a Boston suburb, and a summer place in Maine. But she is not "engaged," as she thinks Louise is: "Well, my mind isn't. Or I'm losing it or something. I'm not all there is all."[2] At some point after leaving Bryn Mawr, Carrie had gone to California where she met an acquaintance from college days, Richard, a poet, with whom she had had an affair. Later, after a brief courtship, she had married David, a politician.

Carrie is one of Wilson's women of short-lived political commitment. She had tried "to solve the world's problems," but now she no longer crusades, since it would seem hypocritical with so many rich friends. She naively believes she is revealing something when she confides to Louise that "the country isn't run quite the way you thought it" (19). Clearly, she has experienced some disillusionment in regard to her husband's principles. As the play ends, both women

are morosely inebriated, and they sit, trying to comfort each other
with words that are fragments of futility.

The technique of stripping away the veneer of a character to reveal
an unattractive essence is not new, nor is the theme of failure
wrapped in the garments of success. To make this effective theater,
Wilson adds two dimensions to an otherwise straightforward, realistic play: asides and symbolism. What is unusual about the asides
is that they are heard not only by the audience but also by the other
character about whom they are often uncomplimentary. For example, Louise and Carrie are drinking brandy:

> Louise: Another?
> Carrie: Just a bit. (Shrug to the audience.)
> Louise: (To the audience.) Drinks like a sieve.
>   Always has. Wouldn't admit it on a stack of
>   bibles. Always was a prig. (11)

At one point, Louise apologizes for having responded to a remark
Carrie has addressed to the audience. These asides, particularly
Louise's, are sophisticated and funny. When the audience learns that
the "confidence" directed to them may also be heard by the other
character, an unusual three-way relationship is created.

Wilson's symbolism involves astronomy. Orion, named after a
mythic Greek hunter who wears a lionskin and sword and carries a
club, may be the most famous of the constellations. Nebula ("mist")
is an astronomical term for a mass of matter, cloudlike in appearance
and often luminous. Most nebulae cannot be seen by the naked eye,
but the best known and most conspicuous is the Great Orion nebula,
the center star in the perpendicular triad that makes up the sword
of Orion. The astronomical imagery and symbolism is introduced
when Carrie inquires about the "green" building that can be seen
from Louise's apartment. When Louise tells her it is the famous
Hayden Planetarium, Carrie responds, "I don't think I like it" (10).
Clearly Louise's answer has set off a disturbing chain of recollection,
which ultimately leads into a discussion of Carrie's ex-lover, Richard,
who had gone to California after he learned, to his shock, that the
sun would "burn up in about a billion years or two" (20). It was
in California that Carrie had learned from Richard about the constellations and how to recognize Andromeda, Orion, and several

others. The Great Nebula, she tells Louise, is "a lot of hydrogen gas that's lit up by a couple of stars behind it somewhere," and it will "keep getting more and more compact and hotter and smaller" until it becomes a star (21).

The nebula may be a metaphor for the unfulfilled lives of the two women who, for all their success, are unsatisfied and incomplete and, as they age, are still *becoming* as opposed to having *arrived*. The fuzzy nature of the nebula parallels the bewilderment and frustration of the two ("I'm a little fuzzy," says Louise [23]), who are figuratively lost in stargazing even as they face the truth about themselves.

Finally, the nebula, as a distant star in the process of being born, is a retreat, a sanctuary from the disappointment and disillusionments of life. Maybe, Louise suggests through tears, Carrie's husband will build them a rocket ship, and they can fly off to the Great Nebula. David is "a terrible carpenter," Carrie replies, and only spends time in the shop "because he can't understand why I'm always in such a foul mood" (25). Indeed, Carrie does not even want to go back to Boston. "What are we going to do?" she asks. "I don't know. I've not known for six goddamned years," Louise replies, obviously referring to the years without Phyllis (24).

Their emotional investment in life has simply not paid a very high rate of interest. Romantic love in its various forms has eluded them, and monetary or professional success has brought them no satisfaction. They are aware of "time's winged chariot"; Louise notices that Carrie has to wear a girdle to contain her figure, and Carrie remarks to the audience that it is "almost tragic" to see someone who was once unusually attractive and realize how very little remains when vitality and youth are gone.

The Great Nebula in Orion is a highly skillful study of disillusionment and aging. Wilson's two college chums, now in their mid-thirties, envy the heavens, evolving to fullness over eons of time, while mortals age rapidly. As they take stock of what they have, agreeing that "we're better off than most," they contemplate the irony of their situation (25).

Brontosaurus

In 1977, the Circle Repertory Company introduced "The Late Show," a format for short plays to be given at 11:00 P.M. after the evening's major presentation. Wilson's *Brontosaurus* was the first

production in this series. A three-character play in five scenes, it
calls for very simple staging with only a few properties and scene
changes marked by lighting. Although it is an interesting character
study of two people representing two generations and two different
views of life, it does not seem very successful in its present form.

Brontosaurus deals with an affluent New York antique dealer who
invites her nephew, whom she does not know, to stay in her apartment (which has "one of the ten most beautiful rooms in the city")[3]
while he attends New York University. She had once known "the
Everybodys who were Anybodys" (7). Now, at forty-five, she is still
vital and feels a need for company: "I've got to talk to someone,"
she announces (5). The Nephew (none of the characters are given
names) arrives in the humid dog days of August and is, his aunt
discovers, disappointingly bland and unresponsive. It is soon clear
that although their lives may intersect, they will never really interact. The young man realizes that he is unable to provide the
"nourishment" she needs. After a few weeks, he decides to move
out and live with some of his friends.

The third character, the Dealer's Assistant, a woman of approximately the same age (who spends all her time polishing a silver
candlestick), seems little more than another voice for her employer,
a device to avoid having the Dealer talk to herself or the audience.
There is little action in the play, although there is, on the part of
the aunt and nephew, some interesting character revelation.

The Dealer is searching not just for someone to talk to and be
with but also for something to believe in. She describes herself as
an innocent with a "virgin streak" who still believes, or has "a
desperate need to believe," or maybe not a need but just "an enor-
mous welling hope." This attitude consigns her to a "moral ado-
lescence," she suspects, but it accounts for her invitation to her
nephew (5). Although her apartment has been photographed many
times, "in not one picture has there been a living soul" (8).

As weeks pass, the Dealer finds that the generation gap is not
closing, that, in fact, the Nephew gives her "the feeling of being
one of {Jean} Tinguely's antique-looking, non-product-producing
machines. Something useless and archaic and mildly amusing and
above all something that makes a great deal of noise as it clanks
around in its useless revolution" (10). Having invited him to bring
joy into her life, to be "someone who would listen, not someone
who would only wait till I had finished" (11), she finds that after

a few weeks he merely wishes to leave her. The fourth (and most important) scene dramatizes their basic conflict, as the two describe their very different mystical or quasi-religious experiences, which indicate not only a generational gap but also a philosophical one.

Early in the play, the Nephew tells his aunt that he plans to study theology. Later, he describes in detail (he has up till then been quite reticent and laconic) how he arrived at this decision as a result of an experience at the age of twelve when "the hand of God reached out and touched me." This transcendent encounter made him feel as though he had been "changed into a gas"; he heard people speaking in languages that he understood but had never heard; he knew about places he had never visited; and he was transformed into people of other sexes, ages, and nationalities. His description of all this in his only long speech is very graphic while conveying a sense of the mystery. "After that," he concludes, "I decided to study theology" (14).

While the Nephew seems smug in his "unshakable" commitment to theology, the Dealer has sublimated religion into art ("The Protestant Ethic with taste," she calls it, or "maybe it should be the Protestant Aesthetic" [14]). She is "shakable to the core," she says (14), suspicious of an easy philosophy and skeptical of "anyone who has it all so worked out" (16). In her most important speech, she attacks his view of life ("a kind of promiscuous protoplasmic soup") and insists she cannot put aside the vanity of the world so easily, being "hopelessly *involved* " with it. She is of that generation of "honorable brontosaurs" who "plugged away those last few weeks before everlasting life was discovered" and "bumbled glassy-eyed . . . through life's humiliating, predictable metamorphoses . . . with a semblance of grace and compassion" (18–19). The Nephew (Wilson says) "is trying to find a way to help her," but she urges him to leave (19). His view of life, his "theology," is sterile, and her indictment of him as "smug, simpering, sentimental, asinine, sophomoric" is not unfair (19).

At the end of the play, she assures the Assistant that "there's no talking with someone who has seen the light. Unless one has also seen the light" (19). In these final moments, there are subtle echoes of the New Testament, John Donne, Dylan Thomas, and Tennessee Williams. As the Dealer sends her helper home for the day, she lights a symbolic candle, for indeed she has seen a light of her own. Then after her last line, she blows it out. "And whatever is happening to me, I'm not afraid," she says firmly, a brontosaurus still "involved" with life even though facing extinction (20).

Brontosaurus examines a type of character who is biologically sterile but fertile and regenerative in her involvement with art and with the *"stuff* we are all made from" (17). The play condems the successors of the flower children, who, having worked it all out, find little in life that is joyous and vital. There are some very fine speeches, and the character of the Dealer is well drawn and funny. "We should feel a power and a danger" in the Nephew, the playwright says, but neither quality informs his stance or his lines (7). Aside from his description of the mystical visitation from God, he is bland and uninteresting. *Brontosaurus* is long-winded and somewhat murky in its philosophy. There has been speculation that Wilson might rework it into something quite different.

Bar Play

In 1978, Wilson wrote *Bar Play* (still unpublished) for the Actors Company of Louisville, Kentucky. Although he labels the piece a "10 minute play" (it probably runs between fifteen and twenty minutes), he warns it should not be rushed but played at a very "natural speed for a desultory afternoon."[4] *Bar Play* is set in a downtown bar of a rather large city on Labor Day afternoon. The characters are given no names; they are a middle-aged Cabdriver, a Bartender and a Waitress in their thirties, and a Sportsfan of "any age." A television set is a fifth character and hangs over their heads, perhaps on the "fourth wall" of a setting that may be detailed and realistic or quite minimal, involving only a bar and a few stools.

Like Wilson's *Hot-l Baltimore, Bar Play* is set in a semipublic place where a variety of people gather. It is also a play in which characters talk to each other without really communicating, although their conversations sometimes converge with comic or ironic effect. As the four talk, they casually watch television and comment on a Labor Day parade in Phoenix, Arizona, that is beset by rain. The Sportsfan, probably the least important of the four, remarks caustically on the parade ("Who is that broad? Makin' like Bess Meyerson?") as he waits for the major sports attraction to begin. The Waitress dreams aloud of the floor shows she and a friend will stage at a supper club to be opened "out on the turnpike." (The first show is to have a Washington-and-the-cherry-tree theme.)

The Cabdriver complains of "slow business" on the holiday afternoon but soon turns to praising his fourteen-year-old daughter, a subject that apparently does not interest the other three, although he reminds them that he had once brought the girl into the bar with him. The Bartender, both social critic and lady's man, seems evasive about the cabbie's daughter, although the cabbie insists the girl has spoken of him. Later the Barman needles the Cabdriver by suggesting the daughter might sing in the projected supper club floor show with the Washington theme: "Hey, think your daughter would make a good cherry tree? . . . I'd sure volunteer to chop her down, I'll tell you." Then the Waitress remembers she heard the girl sing in the bar once, but she too turns evasive when the cabbie-father asks when this happened.

When he is baited further, the Cabdriver demands to know what the Barman knows about his daughter, and when he attacks the Barman, he is knocked down. "Ask him what he knows about my kid," the cabbie demands from the floor. "You don't want to know what I know," replies the Bartender as he leaves. When the father protests that his daughter is only fourteen, the tough Waitress cautions him: "Honey, I wouldn't want to tell you what I was doin' when I was fourteen." The play ends with the television announcer's jaunty remark that "it's a beautiful day for a game."

Ironically, a rather ugly little game has briefly been played here: the father's boasting about his daughter—the "light of my life," he calls her, "the best professional singer you'll ever hear"—finally tempts both the Barman and the Waitress to imply that the girl has come to the bar alone. The Barman hints at some unpleasant knowledge of her, but what? Is he, with the help of the Waitress, merely tormenting the father? Out of irritation or envy or perhaps out of annoyance that a father would introduce his fourteen-year-old daughter into a bar? There is a Pinteresque sense of mystery here, for the facts remain unknown.

The Barman plays social critic when he remarks that his customers search for an escape mechanism: "They're all lookin' for somethin' to forget they're workin' for nuthin'." The disillusionment of an idolizing father begins, appropriately on Labor Day, when he discovers that the daughter he works for ("only thing held our marriage together") may turn out to be "nuthin'." Like some of Wilson's Hotel Baltimore residents, the Bartender points out that people seek illusions, even temporary ones, to make them feel that the future holds promise and purpose. *Bar Play* is a typical Wilson one-act play, realistic, subtle, and quite effective.

Chapter Eleven
The Hot-l Baltimore

In the tradition of the Circle Repertory Company, Wilson had been given a date by which to have a new play ready. "So I told myself that I have this idea, it's just so tentative. . . . It's like a long, aching lament for the lost railroads because I'm a railroad freak. . . . The next day I started working on this play that would take place in a hotel right next to the railroad tracks."[1]

The play did not go well at first. It sounded too much like *Balm in Gilead*—in fact, it was the same hotel that figured briefly in that earlier work. Then it became clear that a railroad engineer was somehow involved. Still, nothing worked until a character named April appeared. Millie, who was based on a waitress Wilson had known in Chicago, was already in the plot (she had also appeared in the first play Wilson wrote), and she helped to establish the tone he was looking for.

After Millie's first scene with the Girl, Wilson was not sure what would happen next. "But when April came into the play, I said, alright, what is it? She's a prostitute. I know exactly what this hotel is: it's a prostitute's hotel; it's half prostitutes and half elderly people. I'd seen that in Chicago. . . . And then it flew from there on."[2]

The first act took a month; the second act, two; but Wilson was puzzled as to what would happen in the third act. He had to "wind up about five different stories," and there was also the question of the tone for act 3: "I deliberately tried to have a positive statement at the end of this play, so I set it in spring—all comedy is supposed to be in the spring. I read *The Cherry Orchard,* and that ends with them all having champagne. . . . As soon as I said 'champagne,' I said, Suzy is leaving. She's found herself a John. . . . there's a party—it's as simple as can be. That's where I got the idea. . . . In spring you have to have the wine ritual, and in a comedy you have to celebrate the harvest."[3]

The Hot-l Baltimore—the play lacked a title until the first rehearsal—opened at the Circle Repertory Theatre on upper Broadway on 4 February 1973. Later it was transferred to the Circle-in-the-

Square in Greenwich Village, where it ran for 1,166 performances. *Hot-l* is probably the play most responsible for making Wilson's reputation as one of America's leading young playwrights, and it focused national attention on the Circle Repertory Company. The rights were subsequently purchased for a television series, which in Wilson's view was "a disaster." When his offer to help was rejected, he washed his hands of the project, and the series died quietly.

Plot

The Hot-l Baltimore comes dangerously close to being plotless; in this respect, it is very similar to *Balm in Gilead.* Stylistically, it is far less experimental, for it is pure realism. Since it is in the tradition of plays set in public or semipublic places, it presents both hotel employees and hotel residents, as well as some outsiders. It is three one-act slices of life as lived during what may be the last months of a once grand but now run-down hotel in Baltimore, near the railway terminal, on a Memorial Day Monday, probably early in the 1970s.

Act 1 is set at 7:30 in the morning. The night desk clerk, Bill Lewis, is making wake-up calls and arguing with two resident prostitutes, the Girl and April Green. The Girl discovers a stack of eviction notices: the hotel is to be torn down and the residents are being given thirty days to move out. A minor character, Mrs. Bellotti, awaits the manager to try to talk him into allowing her son to return to the hotel after a stay in jail. Millie, a retired waitress, comes down to the lobby to read the paper. Jackie, a young lesbian, and her younger teenage brother, Jamie, also wait to speak with the manager. Suzy, a third prostitute, returns with a john who later locks her out of her room and leaves. She creates a disturbance when she appears in the lobby, wearing nothing but a towel, to denounce the departing john. Young Paul Granger III, who has been sleeping in a chair since 4:00 A.M., awakens to accuse the hotel of being a "goddamned flophouse."

That afternoon (act 2), Paul nags the day desk clerk into helping him try to trace his grandfather who more than a year before had lived at the hotel and has since disappeared. Jamie and an older resident, Mr. Morse, kill time by playing checkers and fall to quarreling and fighting. Millie describes her girlhood in a big Victorian house in Baton Rouge and fascinates the Girl with her stories of ghosts. The Girl, a railroad buff, learns Paul's grandfather was a railroad engineer and immediately offers to help him go through hotel records to try to locate a forwarding address. Jackie had earlier insisted on adjusting Mr. Morse's window when he complained his room was too cold; now he appears claiming he has been robbed. She is searched, the stolen jewelry is found, and she and her brother are told to leave that evening.

At midnight (act 3), April recounts to Bill her evening's adventures with an assortment of johns. The Girl searches through hotel records for information on Paul's grandfather. Jamie has waited all evening for his sister who has gone to "get gas" for their car. Suzy comes down with her luggage, announcing that she is moving out of the hotel because she has found a "friend" and protector. When Paul returns, the Girl tells him she has located his grandfather's name in hotel records, but the young man is no longer interested. Suzy reappears with champagne, and they all toast her new life, suspecting it will not last long and that she will soon be moving back in. She leaves in a taxi, as April tries to cheer up Jamie.

Theme and Setting

In 1957, Wilson went to Chicago where he worked as an artist in an advertising agency. "I got to Chicago just as they were tearing down every Frank Lloyd Wright building they could get their hands on," he remembers. "There would be a dozen ugly buildings in a row, and they would tear down the brilliant Frank Lloyd Wright building for a parking lot."[4] The impetus, the theme, and the symbolism of *The Hot-l Baltimore* grew out of Wilson's revulsion at the way contemporary America was devouring its artistic heritage to make room for the modern and the mediocre. The Hotel Baltimore, which may be the next victim of urban renewal, was "an elegant and restful haven" with marble stairs and floors, carved wood paneling, and bronze chandeliers. Once gracious, it has aged through neglect, and now it is marked for demolition.

The Hot-l Baltimore is a threnody for an era of building grandly for a nation's and a society's future, building with a vision that would sustain the mind and spirit, commemorate the best of what had been, and inspire something even better in days to come. That vision, however, had dissipated through changing values and economic fluctuations. "Baltimore used to be one of the most beautiful cities in America," sighs the Girl. "Every city in America used to be one of the most beautiful cities in America," responds April.[5]

Why Baltimore? Wilson had two reasons: "Baltimore is the epitome, to me, of a city that was once really great and is now going to hell in a handbag."[6] It is a case of urban sprawl that resulted in a city grown so large so rapidly that the spirit withered in what had been the very core of its being, its heart, literally and figuratively. In this sense, Baltimore is not much different from other major American cities—Boston and Detroit, for example—affected by the same blight.

Wilson's second reason is probably more important: "Baltimore," he reminded an interviewer, "was once the first railway center in this country. . . . That's why the lament for the railroad goes through the play."[7] The playwright, a self-proclaimed "railroad freak," like the Girl, liked to listen to trains in his youth and could identify them by their whistles, and he strongly resented the neglect into which rail service had fallen by the 1970s. The decline of the railroad was followed by the decline of facilities that served railway passengers. "Once there was a railroad" is the elegiac way he begins "The Scene," in *The Hot-l Baltimore,* suggesting, as in a fairy tale, a vanished era, a golden age of travel (xiii).

The set has three main areas of action; all are in the hotel lobby and all are ugly and scarred by time and use: (1) the front desk, situated so the audience can see both before and behind it; (2) the lounge, with ugly, modern furniture; and (3) the once-grand marble staircase curving up into darkness, necessary as never before, since the elevator does not work. These three areas stand like "the remains of a building already largely demolished" (xiii).

A "Rivera-style mural" over the front desk of the westward progress of the railroads is a mocking reminder of high hopes and golden prospects. A small, cheap radio is the means of incorporating contemporary music into the setting. Heard before the play and at intermissions, the music is to be "a positive song with an upbeat" to match the mood of the first and third acts.

Since the play commemorates establishments and institutions of the past, it is appropriate that the time of the action is Memorial Day. It is worth noting too that the playwright adheres to the classical unity of time, with the three acts taking place at morning, afternoon, and midnight.

The most likely literary ancestor of *The Hot-l Baltimore* is Maxim

Gorki's *The Lower Depths,* set in a flophouse for down-and-outers. In American drama, there is Eugene O'Neill's *The Iceman Cometh,* with its assembly of drunks who find solace only in "pipedreams," the bottle, and death. And there is also William Saroyan's *The Time of Your Life,* with its collection of blowsy, warm-hearted ne'er-do-wells who pass through a San Francisco bar. In style and tone, Wilson's play seems indebted to Saroyan's, and several of his *Hot-l* characters might fairly be described as Saroyanesque.

Characters: "A Beef or a Goal"

"I always start with a character who has a beef or a goal,"[8] Wilson once said when discussing play-writing. The characters who live in, work in, or visit the Hotel Baltimore may be divided into three groups: those who have goals and perhaps a real "beef" or two, characters like the Girl, Jackie, Paul Granger III, Suzy, and even Mrs. Belotti. Millie and April fall in a special second group, characters who neither strive for something nor get upset by what life brings them. The characters in a third group have only responsibilities and complaints, not goals or "beefs." They are Jamie (who has not yet become his own man), Mr. Morse, Mr. Katz, Mrs. Oxenham, and Bill Lewis. The last three are fixtures, almost like furnishings, of the Hotel Baltimore.

The Girl

The Girl clearly speaks for the playwright. In the first two or three minutes of the play, she introduces the theme of destruction: "That was such a beautiful place!" she says of another hotel (aptly named the Pioneer) currently under the wrecker's ball; "Why do they tear everything down?" (5). She has traveled in "every state in the Union. Some of them three times" (80). She is a "train freak" and is highly critical of the disarray of the country's rail system (80). Having precise knowledge of local trains, their names, their schedules, and even the condition of the roadbeds, she is highly annoyed when they run late and once sent a congratulatory telegram to the front office when the Continental came through Baltimore on time.

The Girl is a prostitute, but this side of her character is minimized in the play. Sometimes she veers toward sentimentality, almost becoming a stereotype, the uncommonly decent and unprofessional whore. She likes getting involved: "Nobody's got the conviction to act on their passions," she complains. "I don't think it matters what someone believes in. I just think it's really chicken not to believe in anything!" (140–41). Her goal is a romantic's impossible dream: "I want some *major miracle* in my lifetime!" she exclaims (92).

Although her idealism and commitment are admirable if somewhat vague, she functions very effectively in the dust and debris of the hotel lobby. It is she who announces that she will not vacate despite the eviction notice. It is she who finds information about Paul Granger's grandfather in the hotel's records and vehemently criticizes Paul when he unexpectedly gives up his search. So sympathetic, in fact, are all three of the prostitutes in the play that more than one critic commented on their "hearts of gold." Wilson disagrees: "They're your basic prostitutes, hard as nails. Sure, they may be gushing and sentimental at times, but you've got to give them *something*."[9]

Jackie and Jamie: "Flotsam and Jetsam"

Jackie and Jamie, sister and brother, are twenty-four and nineteen respectively. Jackie, in jeans and boots, has the "manner, voice and stance . . . of a young stevedore" (xii). Her brother is slight, not robust, and quite browbeaten by his domineering sister who is menacingly protective, genuinely affectionate, and finally disloyal. After telling him she is going to put gas in their car for their trip west, she deserts him. Jackie's immediate "beef" is based on physical needs: she needs money and she is a health food enthusiast. She has a commitment in the form of a phony deed to land in Utah, which she and her brother have bought for fifteen dollars an acre via a radio advertisement. Her goal, to farm their own land instead of picking someone else's crops in Florida, is more utopian than the dreams of most of the other residents.

Jamie waits faithfully throughout act 3 for his sister to return. As he dances with April at Suzy's champagne celebration at the end of the play, we wonder if, away from Jackie, he may come into his manhood and join the dance of life.

Paul: Grangeritis

Most of the principal characters have at least one really good moment in the play, despite their compromises and otherwise shady activities. Paul's best moment comes when he tells the Girl that, although his family did not want his grandfather, "*I* want him, *I* have room for him" (95). Despite her energetic assistance, he abandons his search in act 3. It is never clear why he gives up so easily on a goal that obviously means something to him, but his lack of commitment ("Grangeritis," April calls it) bespeaks not only his own loss of direction but an easy surrender of his own personal heritage.

Suzy: "The Worst Judge of Character in Baltimore"

Suzy is a joyously funny and optimistic character. Despite being typecast as the simple-minded tart, she manages to rise above cliché and stereotype. She is thirty, "hopelessly romantic and hard as nails" (xii). As hostess of her own postmidnight champagne party, Suzy has the honor of bringing the comedy to a classic conclusion. Her party celebrates both moving out and moving in, since she has found a john who is setting her up in a five-room apartment she will share with a "wife-in-law." She is thrilled and naively happy. "This is my first *real friend*," she insists. "I need love! . . . I am a friendly person and it gets me in trouble" (132–33). When they try to warn her against Billy Goldhole ("That is not his name," she insists [134]), she angrily flounces out, hoping they will "tear down the place with all of you in it." "She's got to be the worst judge of character in Baltimore," sighs the Girl. "She's gotta be the worst character in Baltimore," announces April, who has the sharpest wit in the play (135). Suzy quickly returns, however, to declare her love for them ("We been like a family, haven't we? My family" [136]). They all know her well enough to expect her back at the hotel in a few days or weeks.

April and Millie: Flesh and Spirit

April Green, the only female resident to be given a (symbolic) last name, is large, very realistic, and bitingly funny. Unlike most of the characters, she has no particular goal and no "beef" more serious than the color and temperature of the hotel water. April is flesh, living, vital flesh, committed to nothing except sexual love and other sensual pleasures. She has no concept of time; she owns no watch, preferring always to go by the clock in front of the rail

terminal, which says 5:15 twenty-four hours a day. (Like the neon
sign for the Hotel Baltimore which has lost its *e,* the clock is another
mechanism associated with rails that is out of order.) She is no
sentimentalist; "trains give me a pain," she announces (29).

Mostly April seems to enjoy life, and we enjoy her caustic judg-
ments on such matters as the hotel (the water is "coming down
with hepatitis" [34]) and her johns ("If my clientele represents a
cross section of American manhood, the country's in trouble" [108]).
Her best moment comes at the end of the play when she prods
Jamie into dancing with her. He insists he does not know how.
"Nobody knows how," she encourages him. "What does it matter;
the important thing is to *move.* Come on; all your blood's in your
tail." The dance floor will soon be torn up, for "the bulldozers are
barking at the door" (145).

April, like her name, is green, vital, life-loving and love-giving.
She is earth-mother/mistress. "April, for all her cynicism, has never
been defeated in her whole life," says Wilson. "She's well protected
with a tough hide and she's trying to teach Jamie to live on his
own," accepting life and mortality but not defeat. [10] The final image
of the play is of April dancing awkwardly with lonely, stunted
Jamie, a reminder of how the lost survive in the war zone of life.

When Millie is told early in the play that the Hotel Baltimore
is to be torn down, she (like April) is noncommittal: "I have no
feelings about it either way. . . . I long ago gave up being sentimental about losing propositions" (6-7). She is more positive on
the subject of ghosts, in which she believes, and she fascinates the
Girl with her accounts of rail travel in the South in an era when
one went "from one wonderful terminal to another" (31). Millie is
not really of the world of the Hotel Baltimore; most of its life flows
over her. "You don't live on this planet" (89), the Girl tells her,
and she admits she has always thought of herself as "a bit outside
society" (31). Somewhat like a ghost herself, Millie lives in a past
of fifty years ago when she traveled on a "marvelous train, very
modern—Art Deco then—chrome and steel," which had luxurious
coaches, elegant dining cars, and a shower ("I'm sure I'm the only
person who ever took advantage of the shower" [31]).

Conclusion

The Hot-l Baltimore is one of Wilson's most accessible plays with
some of his most personal and timely themes. As much as anything

he has written, excepting probably *The Mound Builders,* the play dramatizes the destruction of the American heritage, whether it is a once-effective transportation system and the way of life, both social and commercial, it engendered, or a style of architecture that raised the self-esteem of Americans, rich and poor. *Hot-l* is also very much concerned with the loss of passion that fires commitment, a loss that has bankrupted personal and national values to the point where there is neither loyalty nor love, respect for self or deference to others. Yet, it is a joyous play in which life is affirmed by those who lose its battles. "For me," Wilson says, *"The Hot-l Baltimore* is about losers refusing to lose."[11]

Chapter Twelve
The Mound Builders

Although Wilson claims that most of his plays have their beginnings in character, some also grow out of "nagging little scenes" generated in his imagination. Such was the case with *The Mound Builders,* he remembers, which grew out of two of these imaginary fragments. One scene involved two women at night on a screened-in porch and a frightened child awakened in her sleep. This scene aroused apprehension when the playwright realized that the husbands of the women were out fishing on a moonlit lake and that something tragic was about to happen to them. The second scene involved a wife questioning her husband about "mound builders." He thinks she is talking about a local motel of that name, but she explains that she refers to prehistoric Indians who "left all those mounds that are scattered around." Someone has been digging in the mounds at night.[1] A variation of the first scene found its way into the finished play, but the second one was discarded.

The Mound Builders opened at the Circle Repertory Theater in February 1975, where it had a successful run. The *New York Times* described it as Wilson's "most ambitious work" and declared the play to be "one of those rare pieces of theater whose subject has weight and resonance."[2] Other reviewers, while finding flaws, were also laudatory. Looking back on the play in a 1980 interview, Wilson was harder on himself than any of his critics had been: "I have to re-do that play," he said. "It's just the best thing I've done, . . . and it's no good at all, at the same time."[3] Two years later, the play was still his "favorite by a mile," but he planned to "rewrite the beginning . . . because I think I haven't led the audience into the expectation of that disaster."[4] Early in 1986, Wilson made good on his promise, and a revised version was presented by the Circle Rep. The general critical reaction, however, was unenthusiastic.[5]

Plot

Professor August Howe, an archaeologist, has spent three summers excavating the Indian mounds in southern Illinois. He is accompanied this summer by his wife, Cynthia, his young daughter, Kristen, and his young assistant, Dr. Dan Loggins, who has brought along his pregnant wife, Jean. All five live in an old farmhouse owned by a local farmer named Jasker who also owns the surrounding land on which the mounds are located. This land will be incorporated into a large manmade lake, currently under construction, from which Jasker and his twenty-five-year-old son, Chad, hope to make a great deal of money.

Chad is very interested in the doings of the archaeologists; in addition to seeing a direct connection between their excavations and tourism, he is also flattered by the attention they pay him. He is, furthermore, having an affair with Cynthia Howe, which her husband does not seem to notice. The archaeologists are working against time, trying to excavate as much as they can before the rising waters of the new lake inundate, once and for all, the historical evidence they suspect is buried there.

As the play begins, August has received word that his sister, Delia (or D. K.) Eriksen, an eccentric but respected writer, is being flown down from Cleveland to recuperate from a severe illness fueled, in part, by drugs and drink. Although Chad continues his affair with Cynthia, he is very attracted to Jean Loggins. Not realizing she is pregnant, he tries to win her away from her husband, with whom he is very friendly and whom he had saved from drowning the previous summer, but she firmly rejects his advances.

Plagued by rainy weather, the excavators are not very successful until they make an extraordinary discovery: the tomb of a god-king buried with rich artifacts, including a mask of thinly hammered gold. As they all exult over their find, Chad is disillusioned to learn that Jean is pregnant. Furthermore, he learns that a law has been invoked that protects Indian monuments and excavation sites from developers. The archaeologists had not told the Jaskers that, because of this law, tourist facilities could not be built on their land. Chad is outraged and denounces everyone, including Cynthia and Jean. As he leaves, he threatens that they will not get their way.

Later that night he returns and, taking the precious artifacts, lures Dan outside where he kills him, runs a bulldozer over the excavations, and commits suicide. The bodies of the two men are never found, and they are buried, along with the gold burial mask of the god-king, under the earth and the waters of Blue Shoals Lake. Six months later, in Urbana, Illinois, Professor Howe, now separated from his wife, dictates notes into a tape recorder as he views slides of the previous summer's debacle.

Structure: Place and Time

The general setting is Illinois, specifically an area in the extreme southern tip of the state bounded on the east by the Wabash and Ohio Rivers and on the west by the Mississippi. As in some of his early plays, Wilson has used actual place names of the area (Paducah, Interstate 57), references that point to a three-county area (Williamson, Franklin, and Jefferson). This setting, however, owes as much to the dramatist's imagination as to the map of Illinois.

The stage settings are two: August Howe's office at Urbana and the living-dining room of the old farmhouse. The office setting fades into and becomes a part of the farmhouse setting as the action alternates between one place and the other. The back wall of the farmhouse interior serves as a screen on which are projected slides that document (and illustrate for the audience) the area of excavation. In this way, August functions as a chorus by framing the flashbacks with his commentary and by revealing the denouement. He is technically a refinement of the character-as-narrator, a familiar device in Wilson's plays. For *The Mound Builders,* like *Lemon Sky* and William's *The Glass Menagerie,* is a "memory play," a perception Wilson reinforces when he writes that the house setting "is seen from August's memory of the wrecked expedition and may be represented as he sees it—not in photographs but in his mind's eye."[6]

The play is set in the early 1970s. The archaeologists arrive in late spring or early summer. A key scene seems to take place on midsummer night, and the action extends into July. The group, without Dr. Loggins, left the site on 8 August, Dr. Howe tells us at the end of the play. That previous summer, then, is the time of the flashback sequences. The present time of the play is the following February, when August is sorting slides in his office in Urbana. There are six of these February monologues in act 1 and six in act 2. They are brief, sometimes only a sentence or two, but they provide an ironic base for understanding the flashbacks.

Dr. and Mrs. August Howe

In the longest and in many ways the most important of August's monologues, he pauses over a slide of Dan and reflects on the death of his friend and colleague and on his own career: "A man's life work is taken up, undertaken, I have no doubt, to blind him to the passing moon. I have no doubt that in an area of his almost unconscious he knows this and therefore is not blinded but only driven. . . . We do not allow ourselves to dream of finding what we might find and dream every sweep of a trowel. And what is salvaged? Nothing. Nothing. Nothing" (113).

At the end of the play, August sees in the mutilation of the god-king's tomb a paradigm of man's ultimate fate: change eventually sweeps everything before it, but man still dreams, even while facing up to the final reality of "nothing." In one sense, Dr. Howe is an everyman; in another, he recalls the classic hero who falls through fate and flaw, achieving knowledge of self while bleakly contemplating a future without hope or love. The lines quoted are a meditation on his own life and the common end of all endeavor.

August also adds an epiclike dimension to the play. On his most recent visit to the site, he found that the waters of Blue Shoals Lake (the shoals of time?) had covered the area of the excavations like "a great brown flood" (148). Wilson's imagery of a watery apocalypse in which the house is "lifted up like an ark" evokes the biblical flood of Genesis, and August is a modern Noah as he surveys the ruin of his world (4). Wiping the earth clean is simply in the rhythm of civilization, as humanity and/or nature destroys what is built.

On that recent visit to the site, August recalls, the half-submerged house had looked "more scuttled than inundated" (146). "Scuttled" is a word that now describes his life: he is separated from his wife and daughter; the project of years is in ruins; he has resigned his position at the university; and his esteemed assistant and professional right hand is tragically dead, quite possibly through his superior's failure to be completely honest with the Jaskers. At the end of the play, August stands, trying "to frame a statement," and finds nothing to say.

Wilson's Baptist upbringing may be evident here with its emphasis on the transience of life and the temporality of all achievement. In August's rumination is the attitude of the author of the Book of Ecclesiastes who asks: "What profit hath a man of his labor which he taketh under the sun?" (1:3). Answering his own question in the next chapter, he sorrowfully replies: "Then I looked on all the works that my hands had wrought, and on the labour that I had laboured to do: and, behold, all *was* vanity and vexation of spirit, and *there was* no profit under the sun" (2:11). August's tragedy is not just of ruin, failure, and the Flood, but of the knowledge that the end is ultimately "nothing."

Cynthia Howe seems to be responsible for the photographic slides that document the excavations and their artifacts. She defends Chad's ambition to develop his lakefront property and implicitly defends her affair with him. After the artifacts of the god-king have been buried under the lake waters, she deliberately exposes the film she had taken the evening before, the only evidence that they ever existed. In the eyes of her husband, this professional treason is more perfidious than her affair with Chad. Even if August was wrong not to tell the Jaskers that he devalued their property in order to protect the mounds, Cynthia's disloyalty is still a senseless act that will mean nothing to the materialistic Chad.

Dan and Chad

Dan Loggins speaks for Wilson on some of the larger issues of the play. He confronts the mystery of why the Indians built the mounds by relating the desires and ambitions of the ancients to those of his own time. "They built the mounds for the same reasons I'd build the mounds," he says (22): for reputation, protection, fulfillment, and worship. But if ancient builders are like moderns, then our work—Dan's work—is subject to the same natural forces and the same destructive tendencies that plagued their efforts.

The phrase "vanished without a trace" (which ironically applies to both Dan and Chad by the end of the play) recurs throughout in reference to the Early Mississippian Culture and, in particular, to the anonymous craftsman (nicknamed Mr. Cochise Mississippi) of an awl, "one of the finest-crafted tools discovered in North America" (107). Dan insists that Cochise did not disappear "without a trace" when he left behind such "palpable evidence" of his craft, skill, and imagination. In a poetic tribute, one of the richest passages of the play, Dan celebrates this ancient artist and his work.

Earlier he had quoted a fragment of poetry from another early culture, the Aztec, a beautiful lament for human transience ("This earth is only lent to us. / We shall have to leave our fine work"). This ancient poem seems to restate the disillusionment of August's monologue, yet Mr. Cochise and the Aztec poet did not "vanish without a trace" if they left behind such striking evidence of their artistry. In their examples, the playwright seems to offer a note of optimism.

Chad's view of archaeology is understandably a lay one, although he recognizes that August and Dan are not "doing it for what you get. . . . You do that 'cause you got to do it" (i.e., it is their "calling") (117). But his interest is in the dollar value of the artifacts and the effect the discoveries may have on the value of his property.

When he learns that he has been deceived—that he cannot force an end to the digging to make way for his motels—he is outraged: "MY LAND! MY LAND! It don't belong to your Indian god. It don't belong to you. It's my land and there is an Interstate coming through" (131). Chad simply feels stripped, of land, opportunity, and his sense of dignity. "How can you treat people . . . ?" he begins and is unable to finish (134). Furiously assuring them they will not get the land, he leaves, and we see him for the last time when he lures Dan out to his death.

Chad's motivation is one of the problems of the play. Since he and his father must surely have acquired some experience with real estate in the preceding two years, they could hardly have been so easily fooled by August and Dan or have been so ignorant of laws protecting historic sites. If Chad symbolizes the scientist's victim in his pursuit of scientific goals, he is an inadequate figure. A stronger correlation between the motive and the crime is needed. Wilson is right when he says the audience is not really prepared for what happens, but it is not just the lack of preparation that bothers here; it is the extreme nature of Chad's revenge that stuns the audience, as well as the tragic dimensions of the denouement.

Dan and Chad are analogues of each other: both expect fulfillment from the land that is the site of the mounds, Dan in opening up the past and Chad in building for future profit; both love the same woman; both like to drink and fish; and they are bound by the bonds of the savior and the saved. That the two find a common tomb in the lakebed under the waters of the newest engineering triumph, Blue Shoals Lake, only confirms their symbiotic relationship. Like the god-king and his culture, both seem to have "vanished without a trace," renewing and repeating history in the never-ending cycle of construction and annihilation.

Delia

D. K.—Delia—Eriksen is a fascinating and complex character, which Wilson created to challenge a member of the Circle Repertory Company who insisted she could not play a genius. Delia is a novelist whose work is studied in literature courses at Columbia University. The genius is there, but perhaps the character is somewhat wasted in a secondary role. More is told about her than about anyone else, yet her function in the play does not quite justify so much attention.

Discussing one of her books with Dan and Jean, she explains that she had set herself a simple problem and tried to solve it: "Write a Chinese puzzle box. . . . A box within a box within a box within a box. Every time something was solved, within the solution was another problem, and within the solving of the second riddle another question arose" (102). But she had failed, for either the boxes had to go on forever or there had to be something, an answer perhaps, in the last box. What was in that last box was, for her, a problem in the form of another book. In her writing, as in Dan's search in the earth, an answer seems merely to call up another question.

Has she found any final answers? There was indeed to have been another book, she admits to Dan and Jean; it never got written, but "I heard it—I saw it down there somewhere . . . that graceful, trim, and dangerous leviathan that got away—it moved in the cold depths of some uncharted secret currents where the sun has never warmed the shadows. . . . I could have captured it. . . . But it was deaf to my charms and tokens and incantations. . . . So I went down to find it" (104). Her image of the leviathan evokes Ahab's quarrel with Moby Dick and even Jonah's stay in the belly of the whale, both epic struggles for answers and in that sense like the work of the archaeologists who try to fathom the mystery of the god-king and his subjects.

Conclusion

Thematically, *The Mound Builders* is Wilson's most complicated play, and any flaw in the work does not mitigate the validity of its themes, one of which is the contrast between man's questing dreams and the reality of his achievement. The archaeologists do research that ultimately involves an attempt to know mankind better by knowing what he was, where he came from, and how he contributed to contemporary culture. The dreamers may miscalculate, make mistakes, and tell lies, but they operate on a higher cultural and intellectual level than the materialists. At the same time, the playwright feels he has to be fair to Chad, whose profit motives are understandable. Wilson makes it clear that he wants a delicate balance in the play: "What we should have is Dan and August on one side and Chad and Cynthia and Jean on the other, and Delia impartial."[7] However, Chad's simple longing for sudden wealth is no match at all for the triumph, brief though it is, of the discovery of the god-king.

A second theme is the cyclical repetition of history and culture. As the mound builders created and built, trying to seize immortality through structure and wealth, so do we still seek status and a kind of immortality through building and personal aggrandizement. The play is a reminder that each ascendant civilization and culture has a limited life span. *The Mound Builders* is a meditation on the fate of any society and suggests, in the death and burial of Chad and Dan (and the reburial of the god-king's gold mask), that they too may offer mystery for some future excavators in centuries to come. Finally, *The Mound Builders* is a debate on the issue of discovery and creation versus futility and destruction, and it is this issue that adumbrates the other themes and calls forth all the resources of the dramatist.

Chapter Thirteen
Television and Opera

In 1982, Wilson was asked in an interview how he felt about writing for television. He was very emphatic: "I don't like it." His principal objection stems from a feeling that "you're doing their product and not yours." "You write something, and they change it and rearrange it and do it differently." Their "expertise" lies in making a writer think he is working independently when he is really only turning out a script that will be shaped to their specifications.[1]

The Migrants

It is small wonder then that Wilson has written so little for television. One short work from the 1960s was done on television, but he apparently did not find a working arrangement that would suit him for longer scripts. Then in the early 1970s, Tennessee Williams and television producer Tom Gries called in Wilson to work with them on a project, the genesis of which is vague. According to a review of *The Migrants,* which appeared in the *New York Times* on 1 February 1974 (two days before the telecast), it was Williams who went to the producer with the story idea. After a year, Wilson was brought in on the project, and "all three worked on a plot outline."[2] Wilson, however, wrote the screenplay. Subsequent references describe *The Migrants* as based on a "story idea" by Williams; however, the screenplay is completely Wilson's work.

And it is very good work, much better than *Taxi,* which followed three years later. Like many Wilson plots, the story line is quite simple. A family of seven, the Barlows, work their way north from Florida, where they gather the winter crop of vegetables, up along the Atlantic Coast during the spring months, and on into New Jersey and New York during the summer. Then in the autumn, they return to Florida to begin the cycle over again.

During the play, they experience the harassment of the crew leader, who engages them as a team to harvest crops on which he takes a contract; they work under the surveillance of local law officers who try to keep them away from local towns; one of the family dies; a child is born; a teenage son who has ambitions for a better life finally makes his escape with local officers nipping at his heels, leaving the family with one less wage earner to contribute to the collective income.

The son, Lyle, takes with him a local teenager, Betty, who is as ambitious as he to escape family and circumstances that are about to enslave her. At the end of the play, as the two young people drive toward Cincinnati, where they hope to find work, it is an open question whether Lyle has really escaped the harness of a migrant family workhorse or if he has only fled into a slightly different version of it with Betty, trading old responsibilities for new ones.

The Migrants is rich in characterization and theme. For those who know John Steinbeck's novel *The Grapes of Wrath,* or the film based on it, certain parallels immediately come to mind. The play begins with the almost frantic departure of the family from a small Florida town, conjuring up the image of the overloaded Joad truck setting out for California from the dustbowl of Oklahoma. And there are other parallels: the mother, Viola Barlow, is the person responsible for keeping the family together, much as Ma Joad was. Lyle (played by Ron Howard) is a teenage version of Tom Joad. And the Barlows, like the Joads, endure, always hoping for better times.

Viola is described by Wilson as "hard as nails" with the "tenacity of ivy." Married to a gaunt, wasting drinker, she drives the family from the predawn breakfast she manages to put together until they fall asleep that night. They stay in the always temporary quarters of a cabin, if they are lucky, or in their station wagon, or just on the mattresses on the ground at the margins of the vegetable fields. She is ambitious for her son to escape the only life he has known: "Don't be less than you could be. Don't be less than your dream. That's what I want from you. That's when I'll be satisfied."[3] She is resentful on his behalf when he has to use his savings to help pay for a family funeral, and she is courageously forceful when she must send him away from her late one night, having no idea when she will see him again. Cloris Leachman is very effective as Viola; her work in itself makes *The Migrants* memorable television.

Lyle, at sixteen, is sustained in a life of grubbing poverty by an unbending will to escape. Chicago or Cincinnati is the Mecca of which he dreams, as the Joads dreamed of the Promised Land of

California vineyards and orchards. This will to survive and see better days is the dominant force that holds together the peripatetic Barlows. "Nobody's leavin' nobody now," Barlow, Sr., announces early in the play when his son first hints at escape, but Lyle is adamant that life must contain more than picking beans at forty cents a hamper.

In the final moments of the play, as Lyle and Betty speed toward the city in her old car, which he has repaired, the boy reassures the girl that "We'll think of something." And Viola's voice comes over the scene of the speeding car, softly calling, like a maternal ghost, "it's time . . . it's time," her phrase for commanding her family to breakfast and work, as well as a reminder that time runs out quickly for people like the Barlows.

In addition to the theme of survival, there is the recurring theme of hope. When Molly accuses her parents of always living in hope, Viola turns on her with unaccustomed vigor. "I do," she confirms, "and you'd better learn to stop expecting the worst and learn a little hope yourself. . . . Cause that hope is all we do got." Viola's words serve as a credo for all the migrants: "Well, we'll just have to keep tryin' till we can find somethin' better."

In his description of the Barlow family, Wilson notes that they are from rural Tennessee, so their speech does not have the "popularized Nashville sound." They speak with an accent "much more beautiful and heartbreaking just in its positiveness and in its singing rhythms." His model for their speech, and perhaps for Viola, was the first woman interviewed in the famous Edward R. Murrow television documentary "Harvest of Shame," a film that is a blood relation to *The Migrants*.

Taxi

Of Wilson's two major television plays, *Taxi* is the less important and the more "commercial." He worked on the script in 1976–77, and the play was shown on NBC's "Hallmark Hall of Fame" on 2 February 1978. The script is strong and carefully crafted, with many subtleties that did not find their way into the version telecast.

Taxi is a two-character work, an American *Brief Encounter*, set, except for a few scenes, in a New York City taxicab. The time is the middle to late 1970s, contemporary with the airing of the show, and there are timely references to star athletes and politicians.

On one level, the action simply involves a taxi ride, late one Friday afternoon in April, from a hotel in midtown New York City to Kennedy Airport. On a more significant level, the principal action is psychological as passenger and driver interact and reveal themselves in conversation with each other: their small triumphs and their greater failures, what they have settled for and what they might still accomplish. In doing so, they seem to find a common ground. When they separate, they go in different directions, both literally and figuratively, than they would have had they never met. It might be stretching a point to say they briefly fall in love, but they do part wishing they might see each other again, although no future meeting seems likely.

Serious thematic concerns are as evident in *Taxi,* geared though it is to a wide audience, as they are in Wilson's stage plays. His taxidriver (played by Martin Sheen) is ideally situated to observe the American urban rat race: "I got the whole city trippin' back and forth in front of me ten hours a day; it takes about fifteen minutes to see they're everyone of 'em screwin' up," he tells his passenger.[4] Like the hamsters he remembers seeing on their exercise wheels in the windows of pet stores, people "go tearin' around like hell, hours at a time, runnin' after their backsides." Like the hamster, he drives his vehicle in endless rounds of other people's business. And just as the hamster's wheel goes tic-tic-tic, so does the meter in his taxi, "only the hamster doesn't get tired of it."

The taxi is both metaphor and symbol of the driver's entrapment in an impersonal, mechanized society. It is the wheel-of-torture on which he is stretched in a life that is a soul-killing routine. But if he goes in circles of traffic in New York City, so does his sophisticated passenger (played by Eva Marie Saint). Although she is married to an American businessman who lives in London, she follows a South American tennis star from one tournament to another and has found that hotels and motels everywhere are very much alike.

Taxi is about two people who try to help each other break out of the deadening routine of a loveless marriage/boring job, in his case, and, in hers, an equally pointless pursuit of youth and sex. Along the way, Wilson touches on several other important matters: our inability to communicate, the dollar as guardian angel of the spirit, a deep distrust of the television industry, and the American preoccupation with destruction in the name of progress. The script

of *Taxi* is a very commendable effort, much better than the TV
show based on it that American viewers saw in the winter of 1978.

Play into Opera: *Summer and Smoke*

When Tennessee Williams offered to let the American composer
Lee Hoiby choose one of his plays as the basis for his next opera,
Hoiby reviewed Williams's work and selected *Summer and Smoke*.
But the composer had trouble finding someone to abridge the text
of the drama into the concise form required for an opera libretto.
One night he found himself in an Off-Broadway theater, "with no
thought of librettists," watching Wilson's *Rimers*. "As I listened,"
he recalls, "music began singing in my ears. This author . . . really
didn't need any oboes." After many difficulties in contacting Wilson, they finally met, and "the libretto he fashioned for me sings
itself."[5]

Wilson had never attempted a libretto or even a musical, but he
was captivated by the idea and felt he could do it. "In a sense my
part was easy," he says. "I knew I wouldn't add anything to Tennessee Williams. I just tried to preserve the essence while cutting
the 120 pages of the play down to 35 for the libretto."[6] After
Williams attended the premiere of *Summer and Smoke* in Minneapolis
on 19 June 1971, he applauded Wilson's adaptation: "Whatever he
did was an improvement, I think. A lot of the play is there, and
that's all that matters."[7]

A comparison of play and libretto shows that Wilson made no
major changes and was, in fact, extremely effective in reducing
Williams's script to the spare form required. Irving Kolodin, writing
in the *Saturday Review*, spoke of Wilson's "adroit abridgment" of
the play.[8] But the opera fared only moderately well with the critics.
In the intervening years, it has not found a permanent place in the
repertory of American opera companies.

Chapter Fourteen

The Talley Plays:
Introduction and *Fifth of July*

When Wilson had written about one-third of the play that eventually became *Fifth of July,* he realized that the house in which the play was set was going to be very important. And if the house was important, then obviously, so was the background of the family that built it and lived in it for several generations. Accordingly, he took time to chronicle the history of the family that he called "Talley." The house, he decided, was built in 1860. He identified the builder and established a genealogy of the principal figures of the Talley family and mapped out their business and social involvements in the community.

The locale of *Fifth of July* and the other two plays that dramatize portions of the Talley family history is a farm about one and one-half miles outside Lebanon, Missouri. Specifically, the setting is the family room and the large sunporch of a "prosperous southern Missouri farmhouse," which is situated on a high hill with a panoramic view not only of the nearby town but also of the river valley. [1]

This town, however, is not Lebanon, where the Talley plays are set and where Wilson was born, but Ozark, Missouri, where he grew up. The hill outside the town is still called Harper Hill, after the family who lived on the site and whose older members still live nearby. With the license an artist assumes, the playwright moved Harper Hill and the surrounding countryside about sixty-five miles north to Lebanon to become the site of the Talley family home. He also moved the Findley River, which flows through Ozark, because "there isn't one that close to Lebanon; a nice creek I seem to remember, but not big enough." [2] It was on the banks of this river that the folly, the Talley boathouse, would be located in his next play about the family.

A "Mini-series"

Wilson did not start out to write a cycle of plays, but while he was writing the history of the house, "the characters and other things developed," and several possibilities for other plays emerged. *Talley's Folly* (set in 1944) followed *Fifth of July* (set in 1977). For this, Wilson turned the calendar back thirty-three years and shifted the setting to the Victorian boathouse. The third play, *Talley & Son* (also set in 1944), deals with unpleasant family matters in the big house, while Sally Talley is being courted down in the folly. The time sequences of these two plays overlap, with the action of the shorter *Talley's Folly* taking place within that of the longer *Talley & Son*.

A fourth play in the Talley series will deal with Whistler Talley, the ancestor who designed and built the folly. Wilson often refers to this play and has revealed that it will probably take place in Whistler's workshop in 1913. Whistler (a role intended for Barnard Hughes) will be between fifty and sixty. Other roles will be Calvin, Whistler's younger brother (Old Man Talley of *Talley & Son*); Stuart, Calvin's favorite child and oldest son who will die in World War I in 1917; and Nora, who is preparing Christmas dinner on the Fourth of July in *Talley & Son*. Nora is black and about thirty. Whistler may be working on the folly (or perhaps another folly, since he built more than one). Sally alludes (in *Talley's Folly*) to her great uncle as a happily married man with several children, but he may, in fact, not be married at all. What is more, he may be "a dirty old man." But he is going to be "a wonderful person," Wilson insists, emphasizing that the play "may or may not be written and may or may not be like this."[3]

The last, but chronologically the first, Talley play may take the form of a minstrel show with a mostly black cast. This play would be set about the time of the Civil War when the farmhouse was built. Wilson plans to do these historical plays in the style of theater popular in the era in which they are set. Hence, Whistler's play will be done in the style of early O'Neill, perhaps like *Beyond the Horizon*.

Wilson does not like to think of these plays as a cycle, preferring instead to consider them a "mini-series." When he finishes this group, they will constitute an unusual achievement in American drama, a portrait of life in small-town and rural midwestern society during periods of national crises, covering approximately a century and a decade. He has considered including all the Talley plays under the collective title *The Wars in Lebanon*, because "they all take place in and around or during or very close to the various wars that we've gone through."[4] The complete series, he hopes, will be a reflection of American history over the last century.

Since Wilson is writing about settings familiar to him for much of his life, is *Fifth of July* perhaps peopled with characters he knew growing up in Lebanon and Ozark? "The Talleys are from everywhere," he says, implying that the family has an archetypal quality. "The Talleys are kids I went to school with, and their folks, and people I just knew vaguely."[5] Unlike his own family, which was poor, the Talley clan is "the rich family we all looked up to—or didn't look up to."[6]

Fifth of July: The Social Background

The social and cultural currents of the United States during the 1960s and the early years of the 1970s are very important for *Fifth of July*. The decade saw the dawning of the Age of Aquarius with its celebration of love and drugs. Nonviolent political protest gave way to bitter confrontations, police brutality, black rage, and political assassination. The American involvement in Vietnam became the most unpopular war in American history; unlike World War II, it was neither "sound" nor "just." In the early 1960s, there was virtually no antiwar sentiment; by 1967, a march on Washington mustered thirty-five thousand, and by 1969, seven times that number. In the mid-1960s, draft calls were dramatically increased, and by 1968, there was a major emigration of eligible young men to Canada to escape military service. And worst of all, there were the casualty lists, the bodies returned home for burial, and the wounded, maimed physically and emotionally, who promised to create a second "lost generation." The emotional fallout from this troubled decade continued into the 1970s to plague a divided nation.

Family Background: "Events Leading up To . . ."

The plot of *Fifth of July* is, typically, not very complicated. More than in any other Wilson play, however, the characters' backgrounds are involved and are important determinants of their present condition. Compounding the problem is the fact that *Fifth* is, chronologically, the most contemporary Talley play, with the author working backward in time. So a whole family history is behind the action, including, of course, some matters not dramatized in the other plays, which precede it chronologically. A Talley genealogy appears as an appendix to this book, as well as a family chronology, which lists all the main characters, with dates of birth and death—if Wilson has determined them—and major events in their lives: marriages, children, moves, and other business developments. This background of the people and the events that bring them together on a July holiday in 1977 should help to situate the play.

Aunt Sally Friedman (née Talley), now sixty-seven, is the oldest Talley in the play. A year or more has elapsed since the death of her husband, Matt Friedman, and she has come down from Saint Louis to the Lebanon farm with her niece, June, and grandniece, Shirley, to spend a few days and, while there, to dispose of Matt's ashes. June, one of a quartet of ex–flower children from the 1960s, lives and works in Saint Louis. Her brother, Kenny, with whom she attended Berkeley, is a former high school English teacher, a homosexual, and a Vietnam veteran who lost both legs. He has spent much of the winter in Saint Louis, while his lover, Jed, a botanist, has lived in the Talley house near Lebanon, planning a formal garden on the grounds.

John and Gwen Landis, the other half of the Berkeley quartet, have been invited for the holiday in an attempt to sell them the Talley property. Gwen, a copper heiress, is trying to develop a career as a pop singer, and John, a local boy whom both Kenny and June had loved, encourages his rich wife while he intrigues with her business advisers. Back in the early 1960s, John had fathered Shirley, June's daughter.

So at least fifteen years of living through a hectic age are behind these four and, in the case of the three who had grown up together in Lebanon, a lifetime. The immediate problems posed in the play are: (1) should Kenny sell the Talley farmhouse, thus effectively cutting off family roots in the town; (2) will he return to teaching, something he does well and loves doing; (3) will Sally retire to California, leaving behind her Missouri roots—the house and the young Talleys? The play begins in the middle of these problems.

Plot: Holiday and Aftermath

Late in the afternoon of 4 July, most of the group at the Talley farmhouse are planning to go down to the river to be present at an informal memorial service for Matt Friedman at which his ashes will be spread on the water where he had loved to fish. Gwen and John are enthusiastic about buying the property, but Sally suggests that Kenny should live in the house permanently and teach school, although he disclaims any interest in his former profession.

Near the end of the act, Sally decides that she will not, after all, scatter Matt's ashes in the river; he does not belong on the farm if it is going to be sold to John and Gwen. The memorial service is temporarily called off, and Sally retires, saying she has to be up at dawn to attend a funeral. As Kenny is carried off to bed by Jed, he pleads with him, saying he will not be able to teach that autumn.

The next morning (act 2), Aunt Sally returns early from the funeral, having fainted in the church. Left alone in the local doctor's office where she had been taken for examination, she had sneaked away and walked back from town. June suspects she has had a slight stroke.

John presses Kenny to name a price for the farm. Although he offers substantially less, Kenny wonders aloud how John can buy something so expensive just to keep Gwen occupied with her vocal career instead of her business. John cynically responds that "you can buy anything" (120). Sally's objection to selling the farm brings on a discussion that clears the air on one issue: when John, Kenny, and Gwen had planned to travel to Europe to avoid Kenny's being drafted, John, not wanting Kenny to accompany them, told Gwen their friend had changed his mind. John and Gwen then left for Europe quite suddenly, leaving Kenny behind where he waited to be drafted.

When John bids on the farm, Sally bids against him and wins. After failing to buy the property, John asks June about taking Shirley with him and Gwen for a few months, although he has never acknowledged her as his daughter. June refuses and demands that he leave. John loses a third round when Gwen is offered a recording contract—not with the agent with whom her husband has "set her up" but with Columbia Records. Ken realizes that he must indeed return to teaching that autumn; Aunt Sally will stay in the house with him, and Jed will tend to his garden.

Title and Theme

When the play opened Off-Broadway as *5th of July* in late April 1978, the two *New York Times* reviewers conjectured about the meaning of its title. Walter Kerr wondered if the title suggested that "the day after Independence Day is Dependence Day," because he felt that the characters remained "thoroughly alone, unmoored, uncommunicative at heart." Richard Eder thought the title might refer to the typical postholiday hangover.[7] Both views miss the point, for Wilson's characters are finally not dependent; and although they are literally and figuratively "hung over" when the play begins, they are not when it ends.

The title refers both to the date of act 2 and to the day after—indeed, all the days after—the major national holiday that celebrates not just the founding of America but its founding spirit. It is the day (and days) following an emotional "high"—in short, a normal, everyday, business-as-usual day. It is life in the light of the ordinary and not in the surreal glare of a once-a-year fireworks display. The day following the Fourth of July is a day of commitment not only to the tasks of the first, second, and third of July before the noisy interruption, but also to those of the rest of the month.

Kenny Talley is the focal character of the play, and his desire to resume a teaching career (barely hidden for most of the play under a slightly cynical mask) is an affirmation of reinvolvement with life. He will survive through teaching Johnny Young (note his last name) in particular, but also the younger generation at his old high school (although, significantly, in a new building). His teaching career will be a bridge from the 1960s to a generation that does not even know where Vietnam is located. This bridging of the generation gap is also apparent in young Shirley's rejection of her father. Although she disparages not only June's attempts at mothering her but also her commitment to the 1960s, in a quick reversal, she insists on returning with her mother to Saint Louis, where June will assume her proper role as parent, a place hitherto filled by Aunt Sally.

If these characters illustrate a youth-age dichotomy, then Jed and Sally represent a dichotomy of present and past. Jed is planting a garden that will not fully mature for twenty years, and in his rediscovery of a "lost" rose, he has, in fact, re-created "new" life. Sally, through her purchase of the family farm, has made it possible for Jed's garden to bloom. She secures the house and land as "roots" for a succeeding Talley generation represented by Shirley, who is the last in name, and she "blesses" the garden by scattering on it Matt's ashes, which will quite literally be fertilizer.

The garden, then, becomes a Garden of Life. The return of two Talleys to the land, plus June and Shirley's new relationship, seems to augur well for the family. Nor is the homosexual love of Jed and Kenny sterile (as Gwen and John's will be, since she cannot bear children), for it will bear fruit not only in Jed's garden but also in Kenny's classroom. So the family continues: in the house, which will remain as a taproot for the family; in the floral and vegetative richness of the Eden-like garden; in Kenny's students like Johnny Young, who represent the future; and in Shirley, who will be "the greatest single artist the Midwest has ever known!" (64).

The last speeches of the play bear out Wilson's optimism for his characters. There is no "hangover" here, no disintegration. There is only facing up to responsibility, commitment, involvement, continuity, and survival.

Kenny

This play, Wilson has said, is "about an English teacher . . . who happens to be a veteran."[8] "Teacher" is the second word of the play, and Kenny has the last speech: "I've got to go talk to Johnny Young about the future" (128). This member of the Young brood symbolizes more than just the normal opportunity and responsibility of a teacher, for the boy's IQ is about 200, and he may be a mathematical prodigy. (He is also Kenny's half-cousin.) But his speech is nearly unintelligible. To alleviate Johnny's fear of being cut off or anticipated, Kenny has encouraged him to tell a story into a tape recorder. After learning how to understand Johnny, Kenny has discovered that the boy is very interested in science: the future, space travel, and "teleportation."

At the end, Kenny reads aloud his transcription of what the boy has been saying. It is two graceful, almost poetic sentences describing how earthmen, exploring all the other suns and planets, realized they were alone and were happy "because then they knew it was up to them to become all the things they had imagined they would find" (127). The theme here—acceptance of the future, happiness in that acceptance, and commitment to fulfilling one's potential— is more applicable to Kenny than to any other character except Shirley. The play is "about" this more than anything else: Kenny's acceptance of his past—his mutilation in Vietnam—and his reengagement with the present.

Without realizing it, Kenny has already prescribed the answer to his dilemma well before the end of the play. Weston, Gwen's guitar-playing friend, had told a seemingly pointless but very funny scatological story. It involved a young Eskimo who, in order to thaw the winter's supply of frozen caribou meat and stave off starvation for his family, had broken wind on it in an epic burst that had left the meat thawed but quite inedible. Both John and Kenny condescendingly point out that "heroic actions must have saving results," for that is the "law of folk tales, . . . the law of heroes" (55). Wes is a slow thinker, and the story is dropped.

In act 2, when Shirley mentions that Kenny had been awarded five medals for bravery in Vietnam, Weston suddenly asks: "What was the saving grace?" reminding them that they had told him a heroic action had to have this (97). Kenny explains that in the Eskimo story, the "family was too picayune for a myth" (98). The saving grace would have been *surviving*. They should have eaten the caribou meat and lived: "Don't choke on it, don't turn up your nose, swallow it and live, baby" (98). And this is what Kenny decides to do at the end of the play: to swallow the bitter past and live. By his own definition, his actions have a "saving grace," and he may legitimately be described as "heroic." The Eskimo story makes the most telling point of the play.

Sally

Throughout much of the play, Aunt Sally Friedman is looking for something—Matt's ashes, her glasses—and by the end she has found what she truly is missing. She says immediately in act 1 that Gwen and John are not serious about buying the house and that Kenny will just "have to stay down here and teach like you're supposed to" (16). By the end of the play, these two motifs merge into one pattern, and Sally, having outbid John for the house, has found all she was searching for. When she and Jed scatter Matt's ashes early in the morning on Jed's garden, they consecrate the ground by reestablishing a bond with her birthplace.

Sally is the human link with the Talley past and through her, the family tree may put down new roots. A reminder of her mortality, the mild stroke she suffered, does not bother her; it merely provides her with an excuse to remain at the farm with Kenny and Jed.

Sally also has a link with the future: when Matt was courting her, one summer night they had seen "this silver thing" rise straight up from the river, where later they discovered the ground was scorched. All this happened years "before anyone started talking about UFO's" (32). Sally's story recalls Johnny Young's narration on Kenny's tape recorder about space travel and "teleportation." Sally, like the boy, is "into the future"; the Young and the old are the extremities of the life continuum.

Shirley

As the sole surviving Talley of her generation, Shirley is, at fourteen, a child-woman. With a mother like June and a guardian like Sally, she is mature for her years. She fantasizes about the future and her own greatness: "Certain people will literally have cardiac arrests at the magnitude of my achievements" (64). She lives out her fantasies by watching films of Betty Grable, the "greatest star Missouri ever produced" (33). In Lebanon, her fantasies take a different form; she dresses in her great-grandmother's gowns, thus indicating an interest in her heritage. In the last minutes of the play, she understands that John is her father, and with a new show of loyalty to her mother, she firmly rejects him.

Shirley's lines at the end of the play evoke Sonia's courageous speech at the end of Chekhov's *Uncle Vanya*: "The important thing is to find your vocation and work like hell at it." Regressing again to her funny teenage pomposity, she reminds them she is the last of the Talleys. "And the whole family has just come to nothing at all so far. Fortunately, it's on my shoulders" (128).

June

June has not forgotten, or forgiven, John Landis, even after fifteen years. After Gwen came into John's life at Berkeley, June moved away from the other three and became active and militant in the peace rallies and antiwar marches. She exemplifies the liberated woman of the 1960s. When her daughter taunts her with being cross and angry instead of militant, June is genuinely shaken: "You've no idea of the country we almost made for you. The fact that I think it's all a crock now does not take away from what we almost achieved." She was "something else," Gwen tells Shirley. "You would have been proud. . . . She was ready to carry you around like a flag" (62). On this holiday weekend, June accepts her responsibilities as a parent, and Shirley accepts her in this new role.

Jed

Jed is associated with stability, growth, and the future. He has planted a hedge that will mature in five years, and the rest of the garden will not come to full maturity for two decades. He has been honored by England's National Trust for his rediscovery of a rare "lost" rose. His relationship with Kenny is loving and protective. Even though he is not a Talley, he is "in the family" by virtue of his relationship with Kenny. If the Talleys are trying to retain a sense of their heritage and discover who they are by reconnecting with their past, it is Jed who will care for the family home and put down new roots, not only in the family garden but through Kenny's attempt to find a place in his profession and thereby a place in the community. Jed is a nourisher of both plants and people.

Gwen (and Weston)

Gwen is a marvelous character: foul-mouthed, volatile, generous, loving, and genuinely fond of Kenny and his family. Everything in her life is hyperbolic. She adores the house ("It's only 'Christina's World,' you realized that" [8]) and rhapsodizes over the peace of the Missouri landscape. She is genuinely nostalgic for the years she spent with Kenny and June.

But physically she is "burned out"; hers is a history of "medical milestone operations." The doctors "took everything out by the time I was twenty-five," she says, and she is sterile (50). Every year brings "something terminal." Small wonder that she has "pain" in her voice.

But Gwen is about to turn the tables on her conniving husband, for Columbia Records has offered her a contract. Weston, who seems to be both composer and guitarist for her, says she is "really good." Perhaps Gwen, so vital and earthy, will finally have a career as something other than a copper heiress. Wes is chiefly memorable for his story of the flatulent Eskimo and the frozen caribou meat.

John

A critic once suggested that there are usually no villains in Wilson's plays. Quite possibly John Landis comes close to being one.

He seems to have no qualms of conscience about having avoided the 1960s draft or having deserted Kenny when he and Gwen went to Europe. After marrying Gwen, he used her ambitions for a career in music merely to distract her from his maneuvers with her lawyers. John lives by the dictum "you can buy anything" only to find he can buy neither the Talley home nor Shirley, his own daughter. Kenny hints that he is selling out in the worst way: "I know you're trying to gain the whole world, but what are you losing doing it?" (119). Jed's assessment that John is "sneaky" tells it all.

Conclusion

Even though the Pulitzer Prize was awarded to *Talley's Folly*, *Fifth of July* seems a better, more important play, probably Wilson's most important full-length work. The dialogue is terse and witty; the play has a focus and builds steadily toward a conclusion; the verbal texture is evocative and richly suggestive. There are no arialike speeches; everything is dramatized rather than narrated. With all respect to the valentine quality of *Talley's Folly*, this earlier play attempts, and achieves, a broader vision. *Fifth of July* is certainly one of the very best plays of the 1970s and may well become a contemporary classic.

Chapter Fifteen

Talley's Folly

When Wilson began to draft the Talley family history in preparation for work on *Fifth of July*, he became fascinated with a Talley daughter named Sally. So reversing the order of creation, he made her a mate and began to imagine their middle-age romance. "I liked the two characters," he says simply, "and I wanted to see the play." Remembering the wounds, both physical and emotional, that lacerated his fictional family, he decided that, for this love story, he "should go all the way and make it the sweet valentine it should be."[1]

When *Fifth of July* was completed and in rehearsal, Wilson made up a biography of Aunt Sally Friedman in order to help the actress playing the role to understand her, "a history for her to draw on." He also devised a biography for Matt Friedman, finding in the process that the character was assuming the form of Circle Repertory Company actor Judd Hirsch. The playwright told Helen Stenborg (Aunt Sally) that if she found it helpful, she could think of Hirsch as her deceased husband whose ashes she had brought back to Lebanon. Wilson remembers that when Hirsch came to see a rehearsal of *Fifth*, he told the actor, "You're in the box" (i.e., the urn), and so the central role of the second Talley play had been cast before the first play was even in previews.[2]

Talley's Folly opened in May 1979 and received almost unanimous critical raves. Harold Clurman thought it the playwright's "most engaging play,"[3] and the two reviewers for the *New York Times* called it "a treasure," "a lovely play," "a charmer,"' and "a play to savour and to cheer."[4] The playwright himself, normally modest and objective about his own work, admits it is a "personal favorite" and "more perfect than anything I've ever written." It was awarded the Pulitzer Prize for drama in the spring of 1980.

Plot: "A Very Simple Story."

In discussing his approach to the play, Wilson continually returns to the word "simple." ("I wanted to write a simple story.")[5] The word is apt. Matt Friedman, a forty-two-year-old Jewish accountant from Saint Louis, has driven down to the central-southern Missouri town of Lebanon for the Fourth of July weekend in 1944 intent on resolving his romance with Sally Talley, thirty-one (she says) and turning spinsterish, whom he had met the previous year. After an unpleasant showdown with her family that afternoon, he woos her and wins her that night in the folly, the decaying boathouse down on the river from the Talley family home. That is the action of the play, hence the label "simple."

But as with other Wilson plays, the present action depends to a great extent on the past (see Chronology in Appendix). Matt Friedman had come to the Lebanon area on vacation in the summer of 1943, met Sally Talley at a dance at the Shrine Mosque in Springfield (a landmark still there), and had driven her home to Lebanon that night and the other six nights of his vacation. At her urging, he met her family over dinner; they disliked him for his Jewishness, his lack of patriotism, and his beard. Sally's father denounced him as "more dangerous than Roosevelt himself."[6]

Since then, he has written her almost daily from Saint Louis, but she has responded only once and has not seen him since the preceding summer. He has, however, spoken by phone to Charlotte Talley (Aunt Lottie), who has encouraged his suit. As the play opens, he means to propose to Sally, the first proposal he has risked in his forty-two years. While waiting for her in the boathouse, he turns master of ceremonies and stage director, welcoming the audience and explaining the setting, lighting, sound effects, and the mood of a nation at the end of a world war.

The Folly

A "folly" in the architectural sense of the term is an elaborate structure, unusual and unique in design, quite expensive, and often built out of whim rather than purpose. As they pass the ninety-seven minutes of the play in the structure that gives the work its title, Matt elicits from Sally a bit of family history: that the builder was called "Whistler" because he whistled and sang a lot. (His signature piece was "Una furtiva lagrima" from Donizetti's *L'elisir d'amore,* but since none of the locals knew much about Italian opera, they merely thought him daft.) Uncle Whistler had built the boathouse and, in addition, the bandstand from which music drifts across the river on this Fourth of July evening.

The title of the play also refers to Sally's choice of a husband. Matt, a good ten years older than she and rather alien with his faint German-Jewish accent and Semitic background, was not considered a suitable husband by her provincial and bigoted family. Yet, she and Matt go on to have a very happy marriage, and Matt does so well financially that his brother-in-law, Buddy, envies him. Since we know from information given in *Fifth of July* how well the marriage turned out, reference in this play to the union as "Sally Talley's folly" is ironic and meant to be.

But in 1944, the boathouse is rotting and decrepit and in need of restoration—like the family. At the same time its ruined state is a part of the romance of the place. Wilson describes it as Victorian in style, with "louvers, lattice in decorative panels, and a good deal of Gothic Revival gingerbread" (3). The wood has weathered to a pale gray, and the boathouse is overhung with maples and a weeping willow.

The lighting and sound are to be very romantic, with watery reflections of sunset and moonlight on the boathouse walls. ("The water runs right through here," Matt tells the audience, "so you're all out in the river—sorry about that" [4].) In addition, there are the sounds of the land and the river at dusk: water, frogs, bees, dogs, and crickets. The band, playing across the river in Whistler's bandstand, strikes up a fanfare just as Sally explains why she has not married, and a lightly swinging rendition of "Lindy Lou" concludes the play. To complete a nearly perfect romantic scene, Wilson conjures up the sweet odor of honeysuckle.

"You live in such a beautiful country," Matt tells Sally, and he promises that he will bring her back every year (60). The Talleys may live in a Garden, even though the race has fallen, but it is people like Sally and Matt who will bring restoration through love. The sense of evil, never strong in a Wilson play, is embodied by some of those in the house on the hill. Greed and bigotry lurk there, and evil is latent in the landscape, for snakes may be nesting under the boathouse. But the only serpents who materialize are some of the Talleys, for this is Eden after the Fall.

The folly has all the romantic atmosphere of a setting for opera or operetta. Was there a real model? No, Wilson says, "I've never seen the folly in Missouri or anywhere else until John Lee [Beatty, the principal designer for the Circle Repertory Company] built it for me."[7] Wilson has implied that it was partly owing to the inspired stage design that he decided to write a play about Whistler Talley.

Structure

The playwright is aware that his work is often not strongly plotted. It may be that he is most comfortable with an impressionistic structure in which the plot seems to flow naturally, very much like "real life." This method proved effective for *Talley's Folly,* which seems indeed very natural yet demonstrates on inspection a structural rhythm. Generally, it might be said that the conversation of Sally and Matt goes back and forth between the past, always important to Wilson's characters, and the present, interrupted by several tangential episodes and observations. "The past" covers her family history, his early family background in Europe, and the beginning of their courtship the preceding summer. "The present" dramatizes the final stage of their courtship and their plans to elope that same evening. "Tangential episodes" include, for example, a scene in which Matt "ice skates" on the bare floor of the folly.[8] Also woven into the play are Matt's observations on American labor, the greed of business, and the dangers of prosperity in the postwar era. These references set the love story against the larger, darker background of social, political, and cultural issues of the mid-1940s.

Structurally, the notable feature of the play is Wilson's use of Matt as chorus in the manner both of Wilder's Stage Manager (*Our Town*) or Williams's Tom (*The Glass Menagerie*). Matt addresses the audience in a three-page monologue as the play begins and briefly at its conclusion, in this way "framing" the evening. He immediately tells the audience that he has only ninety-seven minutes ("without intermission") for the story and points out "some of the facilities." About halfway through his long introduction, he replays very rapidly much of what he has already said for the benefit of latecomers. He comments on the "rotating gismo in the footlights," which provides the effect of moonlight on water ("valentines need frou-frou" [4]). He calls attention to the night sounds to be heard throughout the evening. He describes post-Depression America, comparing it to 1944 when the country, like the Talleys, is "in grave danger of prosperity" (5). And he tells the audience that the play they are about to see "should be a waltz, one-two-three, one-two-three; a no-holds-barred romantic story" (4).

Yet, the play begins with the houselights up, and the set is seen in the hard, white glare of the "worklight" that intensifies the artificiality of stage scenery. Perhaps Wilson deliberately calls attention to the contrivance and artificiality of his play to force the audience to acknowledge the unreality of some things that it might recognize the intense reality of others. Much more to the point is the suggestion that this alienation of the audience from stage "reality" is to cause it to be "intellectually on its guard against the snares of romantic love, and then, in spite of ourselves to force us into believing in its truth."[9] This is going to be an easy, comfortable love story with a happy ending, he seems to be warning us, so beware of sentimentality. Then as though to show his manipulative powers, he warms us with his characters and draws us into their problems so that our belief is won.

Matt

Of the two roles, Matt's is the more complex, for he is a many-sided character. Basically, his is a tragic conception of life because of the personal horrors attendant on his youth in prewar Europe. Yet, he can encourage Sally to take a risk and "live for today." He believes in reason and communication. "I have great powers of ratiocination" (15), he tells her, and this helps him to see not only that she is in love with him, but that there is "something to tell" that only she can tell. He can take "no" for an answer but not evasions.

Matt knows he is not a "romantic type," but his mathematical mind (he knows the multiplication table up to seventy-five times seventy-five) tells him his own worth, and hers. He is a mimic, attempting a comic German accent with the same confidence as he "does" Humphrey Bogart or a Missouri farmer. Although he makes fun of Sally's Ozark accent, he denies his own English is accented. He is also very witty and droll ("Olive! Olive! I could not think of your sister-in-law's darn name! . . . I knew she was on a relish tray" [9]).

Matt's most important scene comes when Sally asks him if he has ever been married. In answering, he tells the story of his life, almost as a fable, in the third person, perhaps to distance himself from the wounds of his youth. Briefly he explains how his parents, one Prussian and the other Ukrainian, were "indefinitely detained" by the

Germans, after his older sister, born in Latvia, was murdered by the French. He himself, born in Lithuania, came via Norway and Caracas to America. Because of the loss of his family through war, no allegiances or causes can make any claims on him. He resolved "never to be responsible for bringing into such a world another living soul . . . to be killed for a political purpose" (40). He has grown to middle age, thinking no woman would be interested in marrying a man who would never sire children, not because he could not but because he would not. Thus, Matt's resolution has kept him in a shell.

The most important image associated with Matt is found in a story he tells Sally: "This guy told me we were eggs," he begins, and we must not knock against each other or we will crack our shells and be of no use. Since we are isolated in our shells, we never really communicate. "I told him he ought not to be too afraid of gettin' his yolk broke" (35).

Matt returns to the egg metaphor in his proposal to Sally: "We all have a Humpty Dumpty complex" (49). When he takes the risk and proposes, Sally puts him off. With only two or three of his ninety-seven minutes to go, he looks to the sky exclaiming, "Eggs! Eggs! Eggs!" (59). He is annoyed at their terror of cracking the shell but hoping they both will find courage to do just that. In the minutes that follow, both of these curious "eggs" crack, and their marriage lasts thirty-two years, ending with Matt's death in 1976.

Sally

In his courtship of Sally, Matt has one factor very much in his favor: she does not like living at home, for she considers most of her family to be "hypocrites and fools" (11). But she would never consider marrying Matt just to get away and has given him no encouragement. She answered only one of his many letters and then only to tell him not to write. Apparently she accepts what people are saying about her, that she is turning into "a crazy old-maid Emma Goldman" (25).

Nevertheless, Sally manages to escape the stereotype of the lonely, frigid spinster who secretly yearns for romance and sexual fulfillment by genuinely trying to put off Matt, while, at the same time, revealing in unintentional and subtle ways that she is attracted to him. Second, there is the pathos, even tragedy, of a revelation made approximately a decade before that she must face again in order to give Matt the explanation he insists on and deserves: that she is barren and therefore cannot imagine that Matt or anyone else would want to marry her. This most painful moment is the emotional climax of the play. We are touched by her personal tragedy, but we also know that paradoxically her sterility is the key to a long and loving relationship with Matt. Because she is inadequate in a way that is unimportant to him, they seem indeed made for each other. When she realizes he has not deliberately tailored his story to conform to hers, she is ready to accept him.

Talley's Folly is a notable achievement for Wilson. The dramatic structure is compact although the plot is not very strong. The characters are two of his best, one coming from the playwright's Missouri background and the other created from an entirely different social and cultural context. The setting is functional to the story. The familiar motif of the impact of the past on the present underlies the deeper theme of spiritual isolation making real communication difficult. *Talley's Folly* has been truthfully described as Wilson's "best crafted work," and with its wide audience appeal, it has been his most popular play. It is a major achievement and falls short of matching *Fifth of July* only in the modesty of its aims.

Chapter Sixteen
Angels Fall

When the first season of the New World Festival of Miami, Florida, was planned for 1982, several important dramatists, Wilson among them, were invited to contribute new work. *Angels Fall* was written on commission for the festival and first performed there in June of the inaugural season, after which it opened at the Circle Repertory Theater in New York City the following autumn. The play was greeted with respectful reviews and moved to Broadway early in 1983 where, unlike the author's two previous plays, it had only a short run.

Angels Fall is a very earnest, very moral play—perhaps it is even a "morality play." One critic described it as "preachy," while another called it "a parable." In addition to the moral nature of its themes, it was also found to be "unself-consciously traditional" in structure, with its careful adherence to the classical unities. With a beginning, middle, and end, *Angels Fall* was considered to be "an exquisitely wrought old-fashioned new play."[1]

While most reviewers applauded the fact that the play's heart was in the right place and wrote glowingly of Wilson's language and characterization, some also noted that it seem "contrived" and implied that this contrivance vitiated the dramatic energy of the play. Walter Kerr referred to "an artifice of sorts," while *Variety* commented that the situation and characters seemed more "authorial contrivances than spontaneous creations."[2] John Simon declared that Wilson's "device smells a bit of device." But after judging it to be a "relatively slight play," he still recommended it, and when he reviewed the Broadway production in February 1983, he judged it "the best American play on Broadway this season."[3]

A "Sealed-Room" Play

Generically, *Angels Fall* is of the type often referred to as the "sealed-room play." To put it another way, the "contrivance" the reviewers noted is the "locked-room format": several people not previously acquainted are thrown together, by accident or design, in one setting or situation, and are forced to endure each other's company for a period of time. This device is a variation of that used in *The Hot-l Baltimore* in which the setting permits a highly disparate group of people to assemble naturally. In *Angels Fall,* it is the "naturally" that is suspect. The hand of the dramatist was thought by some reviewers to be too obvious in several ways: in carefully arranging for these particular types of people to come together (i.e., a theologian, a scientist, a humanist, etc.); in symbolically convening them in a church; in adding an apocalyptic note to the proceedings; in somewhat methodically allocating personal problems to over half the characters; and in resolving their dilemmas with rather pat solutions. In short, is the play too carefully and systematically structured?

The setting of *Angels Fall* is a small adobe Catholic mission in northwestern New Mexico. Furnished only with wooden benches and a simple altar, the church is located in the country near a crossroads. A pay telephone outside the church is the only link with the outside world.

If the immediately visible setting evokes a timeless quality, both in its architecture and in the faith the structure represents, the larger setting forcefully recalls for both characters and audience the age of high technology; the action takes place in the area of New Mexico where there is a good deal of nuclear testing going on. One character explains that a "dump site" is planned to the south; to the west are uranium mines and processing mills; waste is also being dumped into the Rio Puerco River to the east; to the south is the atomic reactor at Los Alamos and the missile base at White Sands; and "all kinds of things are seeping into everyone's water."[4]

On the day of the action, at one of the mines approximately twenty miles away, a truck being loaded with "this yellow cake stuff" (42) backed up and broke open a container. The wind blew the chemical over the workmen, and helicopters were brought in to transfer those still living to a hospital. The "yellow cake" is pure uranium, which is refined at the mill. The radio reassuringly declares that the level of pollution is minor, and, as one character says, "anybody not in the immediate area won't get sick for about twelve years" (43).

Clearly the playwright is expanding a familiar theme here; the ruin through pollution of the natural landscape. In addition, the deaths that result are variations on his theme of the destruction of the American heritage. And although the villains are faceless and nameless, the play seems an indictment of a national policy that permits the development of a nuclear program at the expense of both life and the quality of life. For behind the local law officers (just outside the church but never seen) and the New Mexico State Patrol (heard through the loudspeakers in the helicopters) is the ominous presence of the United States government for which the uranium is being mined and which therefore bears responsibility for the leakage and pollution.

In this respect, *Angels Fall* may be Wilson's most obviously political play. The Catholic mission, traditionally a spiritual sanctuary, becomes briefly a shelter from a chemical storm, a man-made apocalypse that threatens four travelers and two local people, thus forcing them to become acquainted as altogether they examine their lives and confront the possibility that the world could end quickly and violently. This new twist on a familiar Wilson theme is approached through the "locked-room format," a device so traditional that reviewers of *Angels Fall* variously cited as ancestors of the play such theatrical works as *Ten Little Indians, The Petrified Forest,* and *Bus Stop.* Sartre's *No Exit* and the "Don Juan in Hell" act of Shaw's *Man and Superman* could be added.

Plot

Late on Saturday afternoon, four travelers retreat into a small church to take cover as instructed from nuclear fallout. Professor Niles Harris and his wife, Vita, are traveling from Rhode Island, where he has been teaching art history, to an Arizona clinic, where he is being sent to recover from "a traumatic nervous breakthrough" (35). The second, more unusual couple is Marian Clay, the widow of a renowned New Mexico artist, and Salvatore Zappala, a young tennis player of great promise. They are on their way to a tennis tournament in California. At the mission, these four encounter Father Bill Doherty, who ministers to the local Indians, and Don Tabaha, a young American Indian doctor doing his internship, whose mentor the priest has been.

The plot follows traditional lines of exposition, confrontation, and resolution, but while all six characters have chances to present their personal stories, only three seem involved in conflicts that advance the plot. Most important is the young doctor's dilemma: shall he complete his internship and return to his home area to treat members of his tribe who are badly in need of his skill and knowledge, or shall he accept a lucrative and more attractive offer that will allow him to spend his life in research. His dilemma is intensified and complicated by the priest's strong insistence that, of course, he must return to care for his people.

Young Dr. Tabaha makes his difficult decision, and the priest learns to accept the fact that the younger generation not only has a right but a responsibility to make its own choices. Professor Harris realizes that, despite his disillusionment with a thirty-year teaching career, he is, after all, a teacher; he is "called" to that profession, as are the others to their professions or occupations, and to it he must return.

Theme: "What Manner of Persons . . ."

The theme of *Angels Fall* is so clearly set forth in the play that it might indeed seem to be preachment. As these six people face the possibility of an atomic apocalypse on a summer Saturday afternoon, the priest raises the question that might naturally occur to those suddenly on the brink of the grave: how ought people to live that they may calmly face death satisfied with their lives. As the priest whimsically refers to these civil emergencies (of which he has evidently seen several) as "rehearsals for the end of the world," he facetiously threatens them all with a sermon. The text, which comes from Peter's Second Epistle (3:10–11) in the New Testament, is a dramatic description of the apocalypse in terms that strongly suggest an atomic explosion. The core of this passage poses a question: "Seeing then that all these things shall be dissolved, what manner of persons ought ye to be in all holy conversation and godliness . . . ?" On the basis of this scripture, a warning of the destruction of the world and the end of time, Father Doherty finds it appropriate to remind them of their calling: "You are a teacher," he tells Professor Harris; "one of those professions, I've always thought, one is called to. As an artist is called, or as a priest is called, or as a doctor is called" (90). Simply, one faces the end of the world—which is also a metaphor for the end of life—by pursuing one's calling "in *all* holy conversation and godliness," whatever that calling may be.

This is pursuing one's own salvation in a secular sense. Interestingly, Harris tells the priest that he "should have been a footwashing Baptist," a term Wilson has been known to use to describe himself (93). It is very tempting to impose an autobiographical point of view on this aspect of the play. Wilson was raised a Southern Baptist, and Baptists believe that their ministers are "called" into the ministry; it is not just a profession they voluntarily choose. Wilson spoke of his own profession in similar terms in an interview in the early 1980s. Asked if he had been at all influenced by the midwestern Protestant work ethic, he replied affirmatively, adding, "if you have a gift, if you have something to give, it's a sin not to do it." This was "thoroughly ingrained."[5]

This play is finally about finding our calling, our profession— our job, if you like. But also important, and reflecting Wilson's own Protestant background, is the second half of this theme: in finding our profession, we are able to face death in the knowledge that life has been lived well, that we have, to paraphrase 2 Timothy, fought a good fight, finished the course, and kept the faith (4:7). Certainly this is the theological implication of Wilson's theme: how to live life meaningfully and how to face death gracefully.

Doctor and Priest

The central conflict in *Angels Fall* is between young Dr. Tabaha and his lifelong friend and spiritual mentor, Father Doherty. Don is half-Indian, illegitimate, and quite bright. He has literally been raised in the church by his aunt who also cares for the mission. At eleven, he had knelt with the priest at the church altar to solemnize his call to medicine. He had planned to be a general practitioner, going from pueblo to pueblo to minister to his people, much as the priest does. As the play opens, however, he is going through what Father Bill calls "his lapsed phase." While doing his internship he had discovered a talent for research and a particular interest in cancer-causing agents. Now he is mulling over an offer to work in a prestigious research lab in Berkeley, California, a position that would prevent him from practicing medicine, thus depriving the area, already underserviced, of his much needed skills.

Father Doherty is disturbed that the young man may follow the lure of money and reputation, forgetting his true calling. Doherty is a lovable character who is on very familiar terms with God. He moves easily from serving lemonade to his guests to serving the host to his flock. When he is angry at the official lies of the government and local law officers (who say, for example, the roads are closed because a bridge is out where no bridge exists), he throws rocks at the helicopters that fly over the mission with loudspeakers blaring.

In the matter of Don's professional choices, however, Doherty is adamant and loses no opportunity of reminding the young doctor of his obligation to his people, an attitude Don tolerates, sometimes not so good-naturedly. The hour of decision is determined, perhaps too neatly, when the road is pronounced clear and Don is free to leave if he chooses.

In their final confrontation, Doherty accuses his protégé of being bought, insisting that he "has been a doctor since he was five years old," that he "has been called" (95). He challenges the young man to say he has been directed to alter his course.

Don replies that he has discovered in himself "a very special talent for research; if that's hearing a call, then I've been called." Professor Harris points out that the priest does not seem to care for Don as a person: "You want that for you," he tells Doherty. "You cannot hold power over another man; even for his own good" (96). The priest then admits that the professor is right. "I was thinking of myself. Well, well . . . vanity, vanity." He nevertheless has a parting shot at Don: "But I'm right, young man, and you know it" (97). When they separate at the end of the play, Father Doherty admits, "I've been too fond." "Me, too, Father," Don replies, and he weeps gently as he leaves his mentor to follow a new calling (102).

Of these two characters, Father Doherty is the more likable and the better drawn. His adversary, Don, is both prickly and reticent; genius is difficult to dramatize. The struggle between them is not between good and evil; it is between two views of what is "good." Wilson's answer is that each must choose for himself, keeping in mind what manner of person he ought to be.

The Harrises: "A Nervous Breakthrough."

There is a quarter of a century in age difference between Niles Harris and his wife. He has recently interrupted a thirty-year teaching career during which he has authored three books of art history.

The Harrises are on their way to Phoenix to what Don calls "a dude ranch psychiatric hospital," where he has been sent, "tuition paid," by the Board of Governors of his college (56). This enforced sabbatical came about as a result of a "nervous breakthrough," which occurred one day in class when he experienced a "crisis of faith, or a disturbance in my willful suspension of disbelief" (35). This resulted, in part, from a rereading of his three books, an experience he found so disillusioning that in the presence of his class, he tore them up and announced that he no longer believed anything he had written. Niles is a man who has temporarily misplaced his verities.

As Father Doherty points out, however, a "willful suspension of disbelief is believing" (87). This immediately leads him to his "little sermon" in which he reminds Harris of his calling: "you are a teacher. So you simply have to find a way to teach" (90). At this New Mexico crossroads, figuratively a crossroads in the lives of these characters, Niles takes new life from Doherty's admonition. In the following scene, he "teaches" by reminding the priest that he may be acting selfishly in trying to dissuade Don. Both men are in positions to influence the younger generation, but Harris knows that teachers should not impose their own ambitions on their students. As he recommits himself to his calling, he finds the priest is his first student. In that he both teaches and learns, is both healed and helps others, Niles Harris is the most functional of the group.

Vita Harris, who writes stories for children, may be the nicest character of the lot. Having been Niles's student, she now seems entirely concerned with the care and feeding of this rather difficult and still quite brilliant man. Although some reviewers of the play pointed out that all the characters were in the midst of some kind of crisis of faith or at some decisive crossroads, Vita seems spiritually and emotionally a normal, healthy person.

Marion and Zappy: Mistress and "Boytoy"

Marion Clay and Salvatore "Zappy" Zappala are the other May-and-December couple; he is twenty-one, and she is over twice his age. Marion, owner and operator of the Clay Gallery in Chicago, has only recently disposed of her late husband's effects, including his studio located not far from the mission. She is not the kind of woman to live anxiously with a young lover, fearful he will leave her. Like Vita, she mothers her male, and young Zappy takes more than his share, for in addition to being a tightly strung tennis champion on the way up, he is a hypochondriac of the first order. He is entirely content with his mother-mistress; if he is a "boytoy," it does not bother him.

This odd pair seem to be in the play both to balance the other older-younger couple and to flesh out Wilson's theme. When Doherty reminds Professor Harris that he must find his way back to his "calling," Zappy, surprisingly for one so young and immature, enthusiastically agrees, recounting something that happened the first time he was on a tennis court. A total novice, he had embarrassed two high school players with his skill and intuition. "On the way home," he says, "anybody had asked me what I did, right there I'd have said, 'I play tennis.' Didn't know love from lob, didn't matter. That's what I am. 'Cause once you know what you are, the rest is just work" (91).

Marion's case is simpler. No artist herself, she has spent her life exhibiting the art of others. "I want to show artists' work," she had told Zappy once, "like Van Gogh's brother" (90). She has accepted that the more modest calling of dealer is as necessary in its right as the artist's. Marion is a happy and fulfilled woman who rejects young Zappy's frequent proposals of marriage. These two characters have no problems that luck on the courts and in the bedroom cannot solve.

Conclusion

Perhaps the playwright seems to urge his theme of the importance of "calling" as the answer to the scriptural question of "what manner of persons" we should try to be. Perhaps he skirts sentimentality in the rather easy answers his characters find at the crossroads as they wonder if an apocalypse is upon them. Perhaps the play, unlike life, leaves few rough edges and unanswered questions. This is the way of plays. Sound construction, a sense of the importance of moral and spiritual matters, and a strong sentiment for people, flawed and fallen, are not bad materials for a dramatist.

"Angels fall, but we muddle through," Wilson has said. People may, unlike angels, struggle, pick themselves up and try again. When angels fall, there is no crossroads; for most mortals, there are many crossings and many roads. *Angels Fall*—the title comes from "one of those incredibly crabbed poems" of Gerard Manley Hopkins[6]—is a tribute to the human courage it requires to look for the right road, the right calling.

Chapter Seventeen

Commissions and a Translation

Thymus Vulgaris

Written in 1981, *Thymus Vulgaris* premiered in Los Angeles before a January production in 1982 at the Circle Repertory Theater, where it was part of a triple bill called *Confluence*. One of Wilson's most interesting short works, it concerns the reunion of a much-married mother, Ruby, and her daughter, Evelyn, a prostitute, around thirty-five, who has recently snared a rich client as a bridegroom. Despite their blowsy life-styles and casual attitude toward easy liaisons—including marriage, these two women reveal a humanity, even an integrity, that is admirable. And they are very funny. Slightly overweight with hair described as "vivid" in color and style, both are comfortably earthy and continually sustain sympathy and interest. Tennessee Williams would be proud of them; they are two of Wilson's most vital females.

Thymus Vulgaris is a California play, although it seems to owe nothing to the period of Wilson's life dramatized in *Lemon Sky*. In the small city of Palmdale, forty miles or so north of Los Angeles, Ruby lives in a trailer "at the smack damn edge of the desert."[1] Her daughter, Evelyn, whom she has not seen for over two years, descends on her unexpectedly to announce that she is to be married that very day to Solly, "the Grapefruit King." Evelyn has come to bring her mother back to Hollywood for the wedding. But the groom has not kept his appointment with Evelyn, and she is beginning to wonder if he will appear at all. A young cop calls with a message for Ruby, but since she is more accustomed to evading the police than being assisted by them, he is tricked into leaving without delivering his message. Despite her earlier enthusiasm, Evelyn has some doubts about her marriage, which is based, of course, not on love but on money and her desire to make an easier life for herself and her mother.

Ruby confesses to her daughter that a year or so before she, too, had taken a husband, her fourth, a nineteen-year-old Mexican named Jose Gonzales. ("It was his first and my last" [21].) Jose, who had driven in on a motorbike and taken her "by storm," was a gardener and a dreamer, and when he had departed over a year ago, he "just took all my energy with him" (21). The unusual fruit of their union is a luxuriant growth around the trailer of the garden herb thyme (*thymus vulgaris*), which Jose planted and which has choked out all the other plants.

When the young policeman calls a second time, he successfully delivers his message: Solly will be "waiting at Schwab's Drug Store all night," and Evelyn and her mother are to meet him there. At first, both women are relieved and happy that the groom has been faithful, but Evelyn confesses that what she wants most is time alone with her mother. She decides to give up Solly and his wealth in order to take Ruby to a little place by the ocean where they will try to recover from life's humiliations.

The play is considerably richer than this summary suggests. For one thing, it represents one of Wilson's better attempts at fracturing stage "reality." When the lights come up, Ruby "immediately reacts to the audience [with] acute embarrassment," not as a character surprised in her own "real" living room, but as an ordinary person surprised to find herself before an audience. When Evelyn enters, she admonishes the stage crew that it "wouldn't kill you to have a step here" (i.e., up into the trailer) (9). Throughout the play, the two women are aware of being observed, and it makes them uncomfortable: "This isn't for people like us," Ruby tells her daughter; "I'm o.k. for a person, honey, but I'm no good for a character." The young cop freezes when he notices the audience, and when he comes out of his fright, he is (Wilson says) " 'acting' and very badly" (12).

This device of "ordinary people" who find themselves "acting" distances the play so that we share the feelings of the "actor" as well as the "character" he or she plays. This double "stage reality" encourages us to accept more readily their rather melodramatic lives and the two options open to Evelyn, both of which are somewhat sentimental and romantic.

The dominating symbol of the play is the thyme that grows around the trailer. *Thyme* and *time* are homophones, thus allowing the dramatist a chance to play on double meanings. At the edge of the desert, youth, in the person of Jose, brought renewed life, excitement and "flavor" (the scent of thyme is important) to Ruby's drab existence. In the year since he left, thyme (time) "sort of took over" (18) and crowded out the other plants, and Ruby has been living alone with "time on my hands" (20). Evelyn notices the smell of thyme almost immediately. She finds it suffocating ("I swear I don't know how you can breathe with that stuff choking you" [19]), symbolizing her fear of time and the aging it brings. Her decision to reject Solly ("Sol. Like the sun. Like Ol' Sol.") and his money (gold) and take her mother from her housetrailer (life lived in transit) at the edge of the desert (an arid place dominated by the sun) to the edge of the ocean (where life traditionally began)—all this is a flight from the emotional sterility of life, especially her own in Las Vegas. "Maybe you ain't used to having money," Ruby says, trying to account for her daughter's indecision about marrying Sol. "Oh, no, Momma," replies Evelyn, "it's never quite the money; it's kinda more like what I gotta do to get it" (23).

Evelyn's retreat to the ocean with her mother seems more un-realistic than her Cinderella marriage to Sol, but it is a symbolic rejection of the prostitute's life, in which love and sex are regularly bought, for a life in which family relationships are important. It is an attempt to redefine and rediscover herself—"getting to re-know the things we knew"—with someone whose affection she does not need to buy (28).

When Evelyn realizes she can—in fact, will—reject Sol and his money to go away with her mother, she breaks the mood by calling offstage to technicians for a stronger light ("I'd like one of your pale amber spots" [27]). By drawing attention to the artifice of the theater, the playwright draws attention to (spotlights) what Evelyn is about to say. There are two kinds of people in the world, she tells us, "the users and the used. Or as Solly says, him being in the produce business, he thinks in food, Solly says there's the eaters and the eatens. And it doesn't take 20–20 vision to see that Momma and me are mainly both eatens . . . But every once in a while an eaten has gotta get away and store up. 'Cause it takes a lotta fortitude being an eaten" (28). It is not by accident that Solly, the Maidblest Grapefruit King, thinks in terms of food, for in matters financial and sexual, he is an offstage version of Lillian Hellman's predatory "little foxes" who are spoilers of the vines (see Song of Solomon 2:15).

The vision here is not merely a predatory one involving appetite, for "past the two kinds of people, past the eaters and the eatens, it's all just meat, it's all just one kind of people and every man-jack of them comin' to a bad end," because there's "no real getting out of here" (29). Money and sex are mere palliatives. In a world of "bad ends," family love and self-respect may be the best to be made of it all. In her last speech, Ruby offers the maternal suggestion, both to and about the audience, that "it wouldn't hurt them, once in a while—just to kinda restore themselves, like you said—it wouldn't hurt them to get away" (29).

Thymus Vulgaris is a play that is resonant with life, thanks to rich imagery, vital characters, earthy humor, and a strong theme. As Evelyn admits, its truisms "come as no earth-shaking revelation" (28), but it takes a compassionate view of the human condition that makes for satisfying theater.

Three Sisters

In the early summer of 1982, Mark Lamos, the artistic director of the Hartford Stage Company, asked Wilson if he would be interested in doing a new translation of Chekhov's *Three Sisters*. The idea of a translation had never occurred to him, but this play was a favorite, and at that particular time, it was a relief to turn his attention to something different. Wilson accepted the commission, and in late March 1984, Lamos staged the premiere of the new version in Hartford.

Wilson did not speak Russian. His initial plan was to commission two literal translations of the play and use these, plus a Russian text, to follow a recording of the work by the Moscow Arts Theater. This proved unworkable, so he had to learn some Russian, at least enough to use the dictionary and, as he says, "be able to read 'Olga' and tell it from 'Act One.' "[2]

Wilson's intention was "not to interpret . . . but only to translate, reproduce." The Russian language proved to be "one of the most melodious" for him, and it was that musical quality he wanted to capture.[3] If Chekhov repeated a word, so did he, and he carefully used no words or phrases that would not have been commonly used in America around 1900. The project turned out to be a labor of love that occupied him for about a year.

When Mel Gussow of the *New York Times* reviewed the Wilson-

Lamos production by the Hartford company, he described the translator as "one of the most Chekhovian of American playwrights" and his translation as "both conversational and lyrical." Gussow particularly noted three aspects of the production that stamped it as a Wilson endeavor. This *Three Sisters,* he wrote, "exudes sympathy for all of its characters, including those who can alienate an audience." He also mentioned a "sense of family and tradition" as the unifying factor for the three sisters and their circle, an attitude often noted in Wilson's work. And there is the consciousness of passing time, increasingly prominent in the 1980s as the playwright moved into his mid-forties.[4]

Wilson's Russians speak an idiomatic English that reads easily and falls naturally on the ear. His cadences are those in which American equivalents of Olga, Masha, and Irina might have pined for the culture of New York City or Boston eighty years ago. Wilson's *Three Sisters* is in no sense an adaptation and may well become the standard translation for the present generation of American actors.

A Betrothal

Wilson's most recent short work, *A Betrothal,* was commissioned by actress Uta Hagen and her husband, Herbert Berghof, and completed in 1985. It is a spare work with only two characters and a simple set. Both characters are, first and last, horticulturalists, specifically, breeders of irises and genuine connoisseurs of that durable lawn plant. But even as we are amused by their deadly serious discussions of bud-count, rhizomes, texture, branching, and subtleties of shading, we are also impressed by their singleminded devotion to quality. In this respect, they are variations of Jed in *Fifth of July.* In another respect, they are like two other Talley characters, Sally and Matt Friedman, who are seemingly unsuited to each other but who are, in fact, perfectly complementary.

Aside from writing and reading, gardening is Wilson's favorite pursuit, and without question, it is the source and inspiration for *A Betrothal.* Only a writer with a passion for horticulture that nearly matches his passion for writing plays could have conceived this work.

The betrothal of the title precedes an arranged "marriage" between two particularly fine but not quite perfect irises, an arrangement agreed on by their respective breeders. These two people meet at a flower show on a drizzling mid-May afternoon in a small New York town or village within fifty miles of Manhattan. Ms. J. H. Joslyn is around fifty, wears tailored clothes, and is totally unconcerned that she is both attractive and overweight. Her entry plant is named Little Soldier, and Mr. Kermit Wasserman had noticed and admired it for its "extraordinary branching and texture."[5]

Mr. Wasserman is as soft, tentative, and shy as Ms. Joslyn is brash, blunt, and decisive. They do not immediately take to each other. He is nervous because it is his first time to show. Under her suspicious prodding ("I thought you were a judge. You have that judgy look"), he reveals that he is an "Intermediate Breeder." His two entries are Big Judy and Little Tanya, the former a debutant too soon and the latter a delicate flower of an extremely subtle shade of orange.

They soon realize that they have seen each other before. She had noticed him at a local Grand Union supermarket. When she mounts a crushing attack on a particular flower in the show (of which she is obviously both jealous and yet correct in her criticisms), he sputters in outrage that she is referring to Little Tanya, his "child." Then, somewhat conciliatory, she agrees that his iris has "a very good color, as colors come and go."

At this point, Mr. Wasserman identifies her as a chaperone for school children who had waited at the gate of a big estate, Castle Crampton, while her charges went inside to see the gardens and attend a concert.[6] He explains that he is one of the assistant gardeners there. As they both enthusiastically criticize the estate gardens for their "tacky little bedded-out beds" that belong "in front of gas stations," they realize they not only have the same taste but the same high standards. They also realize that their plants complement each other:

He: If my Tanya had the texture of your Little Soldier!

She: If my Soldier had the color of Tanya. . . .

Together they envision a future in four to six years when they might breed a plant that will combine the best features of their entries. They could win major awards, be on the covers of horticultural magazines, interest the nurseries, and even make money. Her Little Soldier will provide strength and stalk, while his Tanya will provide color. They even exchange pledges that neither will consider other partners for his prize flower, and the betrothal will begin with a seedbed the very next day. As the sun breaks out and the rain ceases, they reverse their original verdict and agree that "it has been a very good show this year."

Like Jed in *Fifth of July*, these two people represent values that are characteristic of the American tradition of hard work, ingenuity, and imagination. Also, like Jed and Kenny, these two people seem to be single individuals. Their flowers have very naturally become their children. The sensitive and fatherly Mr. Wasserman refers to Tanya and Judy as "my babies" and talks to them affectionately. He has discovered in them the daughters he probably never had. Ms. Joslyn praises her flower for "standing up at attention like a little soldier" during the rain. She has clearly found in her soldier the male in her life. Each has created in his/her flower a progeny of the opposite sex that is, at the same time, a characteristic image of self. Through these children, they will vicariously enjoy the "marriage" neither seems to have had.

A Betrothal portrays a middle-age mating that has everything to do with sex but only in the form of cross-fertilization. This short play is sleekly tailored like Ms. Joslyn, sturdy like her Little Soldier, and meticulously designed. It also has the sensitivity and subtle shading of Little Tanya and her "father," Mr. Wasserman. The play is a showpiece for two actors and a tribute to the skill and vision of dedicated horticulturalists.

Chapter Eighteen
Talley & Son

When Wilson finished the third Talley play in March 1981, he called it *A Tale Told,* a title borrowed from Shakespeare's *Macbeth* and the *Book of Common Prayer.* Since *Talley's Folly* had been greeted by an approval that had built into euphoria by the time the play moved to Broadway, the reception accorded *A Tale Told* was disappointing when it opened in June 1981. Some reviewers liked it, but many were disappointed, calling it melodrama and citing debts to such modern classics as Lillian Hellman's *The Little Foxes.* Nevertheless, the play enjoyed a modest run Off-Broadway.

Wilson is known for continuing to revise plays that do not satisfy him. It took four years for *Tale* to reappear, and this time it was much improved. Under a new title, *Talley & Son,* a far more vigorous, tightly structured work opened at the Circle Rep in October 1985, and although it still did not enjoy the critical acclaim accorded the first two Talley plays, it had its champions. Writing in *New York,* John Simon (who had liked the first version) found the second version an improvement, declaring that the playwright's strength "is in extracting the extraordinary from the ordinary, and, in general, making it psychologically and dramatically plausible."[1]

Plot: " . . . A Tale That is Told"

Like *Fifth of July, Talley & Son* has a rather involved plot, but unlike the first Talley play, this one is self-contained and does not depend much on knowledge of previous events. A choric character is present, in any case, to fill in anything the audience needs to know.

At sunset on 4 July 1944, the ghost of young Timmy Talley returns to his home on the hill overlooking Lebanon, Missouri. Only twenty, Timmy has recently been killed while serving in the United States Marine Corps in the South Pacific. At the time of his death, he was carrying travel orders for a furlough to the States; his brother, Buddy (Kenneth), had arrived home the previous day from the

Italian front. The two Talley grandsons were given military leave to return home for the funeral of their grandfather, the patriarchal Calvin, whose death seemed imminent but who had not cooperated by expiring on schedule.

Act 1 is concerned chiefly with four narrative lines: (1) Calvin Talley, far from resting on his sickbed, has surreptitiously gone for a drive in his son's Packard, knowing neither the gearshift nor the location of the brakes; (2) Sally briefly returns home from her job at the hospital and, finding that Matt has been there that afternoon, setting the family on its collective ear, immediately departs for the folly, protesting she wants neither to see nor to marry him; (3) Viola Platt, the family washwoman for fifteen years and mother of the nubile seventeen-year-old Avalaine, attempts to see Eldon on business that she will not discuss with anyone, but which is revealed at the end of Act 1 when Avalaine (fathered by Eldon) appears in the Talley parlor and creates a scene by demanding "my piece of all this"; (4) most importantly, a large conglomerate, Delaware Industries, has made a tempting offer to buy Talley & Son, man-ufacturers of clothing in peacetime and in war military fatigues.

Calvin Talley is found and brought home by Harley Campbell, Buddy's friend, Sally's high school beau (whose funeral she attends in *Fifth of July*), and Eldon's business partner. Eldon, the mainstay of Talley & Son, refuses to sell to the conglomerate, insisting he must hold on to the business for his two sons, although Harley Campbell strongly urges the sale. Buddy, caught between his father and his friend, is noncommittal, although he, too, would prefer to sell. At the end of act 1, the family receives a telegram announcing Timmy's death.

Act 2 is a resolution of the third and fourth narrative lines. Later that same holiday evening, Avalaine Platt is bribed by Calvin Talley with an offer of a good job for Emmet Young, the Talley handyman and her current lover, if she will marry Young the next day and keep quiet about her connection with the Talleys. Old Calvin also tries to force the sale of Talley & Son to Delaware Industries by outvoting Eldon in an impromptu stockholders' meeeting, but he is outwitted when his son, who holds power of attorney over him, trades the Talley half of Talley & Son to Harley Campbell for the Campbell shares of the local bank, thus giving Eldon control of his father's favorite enterprise. In trading off a company he has nursed to success, Eldon is motivated by the death of Timmy, who had tried to please his father by helping him in the factory and by Buddy's obvious preference for the bank. Calvin is powerless to control Eldon whom he belittles, as much for his dogged industry in office work as for his various adulteries. Harley Campbell, now sole owner of Talley & Son, will sell it, not caring that the factory will be moved to Louisiana, and local women will lose their jobs. So will Emmet Young, who has been bribed into marriage with a job that will no longer exist.

Aunt Lottie, who is dying from radium poisoning, withholds the news of Timmy's death from Sally when she returns later that night from the folly, for Lottie fears it may be the one thing that would keep Sally from leaving home and marrying Matt.

Tale into *Talley*

More than one reviewer noted that the new title, *Talley & Son,* signaled a stronger focus on the father-son relationship of the three generations of Talleys. In particular, the scene in which it is decided to sell Talley & Son out of the family is sharpened to define more clearly the antagonism between fathers and sons. The choruslike ghost of Timmy speaks a prologue in *Talley & Son* that immediately sets the family in clear relief against the background of national mood and international events. This speech and his other very long monologues were all relegated to act 2 in the early version. In *Talley & Son,* Timmy is much better integrated into the action at the same time as he helps clarify it. Avalaine, the wild seed of Eldon's lust for the family washwoman, Viola Platt, turns up not only at the end of act 1 but also at the climax, when Calvin marries her off to handyman Emmet Young. And Sally Tally appears briefly before her visit to the folly as well as at the end of the play, when she prepares to elope with Matt. Unfortunately, Calvin's account in *A Tale Told* of the ghost of a Confederate soldier who was killed by a Union man in the farmhouse attic, an episode Wilson had once thought to be central to a future Talley play, does not survive in *Talley & Son.*

Calvin: "A Dried Up Old Stick"

Calvin Talley, as his name suggests, is the descendant of hardy, Calvinistic pioneer stock who set great store by living a "good, clean Christian life," all of which did not prevent him, as Eldon says,

from spending "half the week at church shaking hands with all . . .
[his] neighbors and the other half at the bank foreclosing on their
mortgages."[2]

His motto has been "See what's happening and happen first."
"You bought everything the war was gonna use," Lottie taunts him,
"and sold it to them for double, didn't you, papa?" Yes, he replies,
"treble and four times," sternly reminding her that his profits paid
for her education. But the war that made him prosperous took his
favorite son, Stuart, killed in 1917. When he is annoyed, he reminds
Eldon that Talley & Son was named for the dead boy and not for
him, and that he has not set foot in the factory since Stuart died.

Calvin is a monstrous curmudgeon, "the craftiest son-of-a-bitch
I ever encountered," Lottie says. He is at once a family tyrant and
a municipal icon, a self-righteous, mean-spirited man and a community benefactor. His own father had died at around thirty, just
after the famous farmhouse was built. "I think," Eldon says, "Dad
lived out his dad's life and then his own. And then mine." Calvin
is an authority figure from whom any son would have to free himself
before achieving full manhood.

Eldon

If Calvin Talley is nearly mythic in the energy with which he has
carved a small kingdom out of LaClede County and in the confidence
with which he has manipulated his neighbors and family, then Eldon
Talley is made of more common clay. His father reminds him that
he had hauled whiskey to Saint Louis during Prohibition days, and
he has sowed enough wild oats to provide a model for Buddy, one
result of which is Avalaine Platt. "Small mind in business and
adulterous in his marriage," his father sums him up, somewhat
unfairly. Meticulous and generally honest, Eldon is, by type, a
"bookkeeper." ("Start keeping books, you end up keeping books,"
his father says.) "You go in that office [with] all those papers, you
know what you'd do," Calvin taunts; "you'd alphabetize them." By
"alphabetizing papers," Eldon has built Talley & Son into a company
worth twice Calvin's bank.

Timmy can testify from firsthand experience that the military
fatigues his father manufactures are top quality, and Eldon takes
pride in this. Timmy remembers that his father always said, "It
makes a difference when you do something right." Delaware In-

dustries, Eldon suspects, wishes to take over the company and "turn out crap." The factory has been his life since he left Princeton two months before graduation (a price exacted by Calvin for bailing him out of a romance). "And it's going to be Timmy's life," he insists, for he had always been able to depend on his younger son to assist him there. But he admits no interest at all in the factory after he learns that Timmy will not return to inherit it, for his grief over his son's death is deep.

When he trades the family interests in Talley & Son to Harley for a far less valuable controlling interest in the bank, it is done mostly to thwart his father and revenge himself on Buddy for his disloyalty in agreeing to sell. That he will lose thousands of dollars on a deal made "just out of spite" is not important. "I can't think of a better way to spend money," he tells Buddy. "You didn't want to get your hands dirty with me and Timmy. . . . Now you won't have to worry about it."

After he has the pleasure of telling off old Calvin ("Dad, why don't you go to hell. At least, go to bed") after a lifetime of enduring his slurs, Eldon bleakly confronts the emptiness of his life: "You just wonder why you did any of it." Not for his sons, who did not really care about the factory, his wife tells him; he was only concerned to "get a day-and-a-half's work out of them." In his own way, Eldon is as greedy as old Calvin, only he has been more circumspect in his dealings.

The Two Grandsons

Kenneth "Buddy" Talley is at the business of begetting Kenny, Jr., of *Fifth of July* during his leave. Buddy is like his father in that he is an unfaithful husband whose extramarital affairs sometimes cause problems. Avalaine Platt complains that he nearly raped her on his previous furlough, and even on his first night back in Lebanon, he tries to lure her into the woods again, thus prompting Viola Platt to tell her daughter that she and Buddy are blood relatives.

Buddy has worked in the bank before entering the army (he has a degree in business administration from Princeton University), and he expects to return to the bank when he is discharged, hence his vote to sell Talley & Son in which his only interest is financial. But it galls him to realize that he will not inherit the bank because he voted against his father, who now owns the controlling shares. We learn early in this play of his interest in prefabricated housetrailers and life in a warm climate. Buddy seems to represent another stage in the general deterioration of the Talley family; after a career as dealer for mobile homes, Buddy (and Olive) have, by 1977 (and *Fifth of July*), retired to California, Wilson's vengeance on a character he does not admire.

"America won the Second World War today," Timmy tells the audience in the first line of *Talley & Son*. The announcement seems premature by a year, but it merely confirms that the battle for Saipan was a turning point in the war. Timmy's appearance in the family parlor is also premature, for he is not due home for another two days. As chorus to the action, Timmy describes warfare in the greater world beyond Lebanon, particularly in the Pacific, the theater of his own involvement; he clarifies the time of the action; and he establishes that the family pow-wow over the offer to buy Talley & Son is almost as important as the state of his grandfather's health.

Timmy is one of the "nice" Talleys. It is significant that he never seems to communicate with anyone in the play except Aunt Lottie. When at the end he, Aunt Lottie, and Sally are all on stage, it is clear that here together briefly are the best of the Talleys for two generations: one already dead, one soon to die; and one who is barren.

Unlike Buddy, Timmy has been genuinely anxious to please his father. "I spent my whole life lookin' for things you'd like," he tells Eldon at the end of act 1. "All the time I spent down at Talley & Son, since I was eleven was just so you'd notice me." His father belatedly reciprocates, insisting through act 1 that Timmy must be involved in any decision regarding the factory.

In a dramatic moment as Eldon mourns his younger son, Buddy taunts his father that Timmy had tried to please him "so maybe you'd pat him on the head—which you never did." When he accuses Timmy of being "his father's little puppy dog," Eldon strikes him. While Buddy sometimes lets resentment surface toward his younger brother, Timmy never betrays any jealousy of him. The core of their relationship seems a vacuum. Encountering Timmy is one of the really positive aspects of *Talley & Son*.

The Talley Women

Netta is a concerned and loving wife, mother, and even daughter-in-law. Much of her pride seems invested in her oldest son in whose honor she is preparing a Christmas feast in July. We never see her interacting with Timmy's ghost, but her retreat to his room at the end of the play signals that she does not mean to be hurt any further by the war. She is loyal to Eldon, but her realization of his infidelity with Viola Platt may have driven a permanent wedge between them. To her discredit she seems to share the family's anti-Semitism where Matt is concerned, and there is little sign of a mother-daughter relationship with Sally.

Olive is a prim and self-righteous daughter-in-law who irritates Netta by calling her "mother" and by being officious in the kitchen. "No piddlin' Yale lock would keep that one out," Netta remarks as Olive grows increasingly curious about the family's financial secrets locked in Calvin's office. Olive is possessive of Buddy and understandably anxious to escape her in-laws by moving to a place of their own. She fusses over Calvin and irritates Lottie. She is reminiscent of Chekhov's Natasha, the dark angel in the household of the three sisters. Olive is also to be pitied, for limited as she is, she cannot understand boredom and insomnia, not even as symptoms of disease; she only knows hard work, fatigue, and sleep in repeated cycles. She is an uninteresting woman who tries hard in a difficult situation. She will always be slightly ridiculous as the butt of Matt's joke about Sally's relative who appears on a relish tray.

"I think the Talleys got to have one in every generation," Eldon remarks of his daughter, Sally. Clearly, Aunt Lottie is the "one" for her generation as Sally is for hers. Lottie cares greatly for Sally who is spiritually her child. She has been Matt Friedman's contact with her niece for the preceding year, and she vicariously lives Sally's curious romance, refusing even to let her say goodbye at the end of the play, knowing that the death of Timmy might prevent her from making the final break. "You fly away on," she says, quoting Viola Platt's instructions to Avalaine.

Aunt Lottie is dying. After graduation from college, she had renounced family wealth and declared her loyalties to the poor. She had worked in a factory in Connecticut where she contracted cancer while using radium to paint the faces of clocks. Then, after working in "some socialist outfit" (says Calvin) in Chicago, she had returned home to die. She is the true moral center of *Talley & Son,* the voice of common sense, and the advocate of romance. She is, curiously, also the focus of a good deal of humor as she sardonically copes with intense pain and her even more vexatious family. Lottie is possibly the most impressive character in the play.

Conclusion

Talley & Son is a family drama that calls up the spirits of Lillian Hellman's Hubbards of *The Little Foxes* and *Another Part of the Forest*. There are also echoes of Arthur Miller's Kellers of *All My Sons* and Williams's Pollitt family of *Cat on a Hot Tin Roof*. In Wilson's play, there is the same concern with hypocrisy and skulduggery in family business and the effect of dishonesty and mendacity on the family. In addition to shady business dealings, there are several other time-honored ingredients of melodrama: adultery, an illegitimate child, blackmail, bribery, marriage for money, an elopement, and a ghost. Nevertheless, since a serious playwright has lavished a great deal of attention on all this material, what in lesser hands would result in soap opera is here refined into an artistic entity of some distinction. *Talley & Son* is a rich fabric of thematic variations interwoven with great subtlety and effectiveness.

Talley & Son is about several issues: the unsteady and treacherous terrain of the father-son relationship; the big fish/little fish naturalism of the world of business; the effects on body and spirit of a long, draining world war and the restless longings for peace and prosperity; the hypocrisy and bigotry of a small town and its civic icons; the exploitation of workers by industry and business that results in unemployment at best and industrial poisoning at worst; the eroding effects of greed in human relationships; the horrors of war; and the courage of the human spirit in the face of pain and death.

The other two Talley plays may perhaps be works of greater distinction, while *Talley & Son* may generate enthusiasm mainly among those who know the other two plays. On its own, however, it is an honorable addition to the dramatic literature of the American family at war, both with the world and within itself.

Chapter Nineteen

Hearing America

There are several key words that describe and define Lanford Wilson as a playwright. First of all, he is very "American." He comes from Missouri, the heart of the "heartland" of the United States, and this background has governed much about him and his career. He grew up in a small town and lived on a farm, which was a common experience for many Americans up to and including the World War II period. His Baptist rearing gave him a belief in God and a sense that one has an obligation to live meaningfully. But the background has proved in no way limiting, for he is neither provincial in outlook nor merely regional in appeal. He moves easily between the rural Midwest and the culture centers of the Northeast and West Coast, and it was in Chicago that he first discovered his talent.

Although he lives in and often writes about the 1980s, he is proud of the American heritage and concerned with preserving it— the land and landscape, the architecture, the institutions, and the traditions. He is a humanist concerned with the individual and with matters of integrity and commitment. In style and technique, he is a traditional writer who is at his best with straightforward realism, seasoned occasionally with a strong dash of poetry. But he is, in addition, typically American in his urge toward experimentation and in his optimism.

To a very great extent, Wilson's art has been shaped by American influences. He liked the best of what he was exposed to in the late 1940s and early 1950s—Arthur Miller, Tennessee Williams, Thornton Wilder, and (to some degree) William Inge and Lillian Hellman. From Miller and Williams, he learned the uses of memory in dramatic structure, as well as the possibilities of free-flowing time. From Williams, he learned how to address his audience directly. Thornton Wilder's work demonstrated the playwright's freedom to throw "time to the winds." Inge, himself a midwesterner, reminded the young Wilson of the rich possibilities of midwestern settings anad characters. Wilson's Talleys of *Talley & Son* owe something to Hellman's foxlike Hubbards (also perhaps to Miller's Keller family of *All My Sons*). Wilson's principal foreign influence—apparent in a work like *Fifth of July*—is probably Chekhov (of whom he is very fond), especially his poetic style and evocative texture.

Wilson looked to the best for inspiration, while not being merely imitative. Just as his style is his own, so in the matter of themes he has also gone his own way or matched his seniors. No other American playwright has written so meaningfully, for example, about this country's desecration of its past. Neither Inge nor Williams has created more believable midwestern Americans than Wilson. In the use of setting, whether totally realistic or somewhat experimental, he matches Miller and Williams. In his generation of dramatists, he has no equal at writing the traditional play in a style best described as poetic realism.

Wilson remembers that early on he was attracted to dialogue, to the "juxtaposed sounds and rhythms of characters," and any discussion of his plays eventually must touch on his love of language and the effectiveness with which he uses it. Speech patterns form the basis of characterization, he has said, and for many years, like Chekhov's Trigorin, he kept notebooks of dialogue. "Not only do I hear the way people talk—and the specific rhythms of their speech—but I have a talent for reproducing that in an organized and exciting way," he has said. *"That* is a talent—everything else is work."[1] His dialogue, of course, is not the way people really speak; it is far more lyrical. One might say (to vary a line from Whitman) "we hear America talking" when we hear his plays.

Wilson's themes are what we talk about, too, for they are the themes of our time, the concerns of thoughtful people of these decades. They are national in scope, particularly applicable to America and Americans, but they achieve universality through their timelessness. He writes longingly of family love but focuses on the individual, the misfit, or the outsider. Such characters illustrate the importance of roots. From "somewhere else," they are displaced people emotionally. On the other hand, the American family, in Wilson's plays, is an ideal not often attained. His family exists in a society that became restless and rootless in the social flux and economic revival during and after the Second World War. It is a society thoughtlessly turned destructive of a heritage it never learned to appreciate.

Wilson writes, too, of the human drive to build and construct and the contemporary tendency to demolish and replace. He is disturbed at the rejection of the old and durable in favor of the new and sterile. His America is engaged in "tearing down," in a pointless and deliberate overthrow of the cultural icons of the past.

He writes of the joys of sexual love and the emptiness of loveless sex, of marriage and adultery, of the vibrancy and optimism of youth and the terrors of aging. He is concerned with the pride of commitment and the desolation of the uncommitted, with integrity and hypocrisy, with greed and generosity. He is distressed about those who drift aimlessly and proud of those who find a "calling." He chronicles the retreat into drugs and alcohol and the courage of those who live without illusions. He attacks the narrowness and the provinciality of small-town and country life, yet empathizes with those who fearfully inhabit the neon-lighted arteries of New York City that flow with sound and fury.

Wilson's characers are both urban and rural Americans. He describes small-town teenagers and midwestern farmers with nostalgic affection. The junkies and prostitutes of Manhattan are as worthy of his attention and compassion as the upper-class overachievers of an affluent Chicago suburb or a handful of frustrated souls at life's crossroads in New Mexico. It is frequently claimed that his plays do not have villains in the usual sense of the term. From a Baltimore hotel, to Central Park West, from a Missouri ghosttown to a house sunk in the sands of a California coast, America is a social as well as a geographical territory to which he lays claim.

In style and technique, Wilson can be highly innovative while still remaining a traditionalist. He was one of the first to make extensive use of layered dialogue to enhance the realism of a scene. He has always been intrigued with the idea of addressing the audience directly, perhaps through a choric character, or in asides, or through a master of ceremonies. He is entranced with the artifice of the theater, the "magic," which tempted him to construct a play within a play within a play in one early, unpublished piece. If a scene is important, he may repeat it twice for effect (the stabbing of Joe in *Balm*). He may write a brief coda composed of verbal fragments from previous scenes all hurled together into a final summary of the action before a quiet conclusion (*Rill* and *Balm*). He fragments a narrative and rearranges it in nonchronological order, thus achieving a montagelike effect (*Rimers*). The past may be replayed by electronic means (the photographic slides in *Mound Build-ers*) as a technique for introducing the flashbacks that form the main action.

Music is also important in the total effect of Wilson's theater, whether it be a melancholy theme song ("The Whiffenpoof Song") in *Louie,* an old hymn ("There is a Balm in Gilead") in *Balm,* a neighborhood radio playing Mozart in *Lady Bright,* a rowdy vau-deville number ("There is a Tavern in the Town") in *Sand Castle,* or the romantic serenade by the Lebanon band ("Lindy Lou") that crept by Matt and Sally upon the waters of the river as he courted her in the folly.

The playwright is equally inventive and varied in his use of setting. Some of the short plays are performed on a bare stage with minimal props, while many settings *(Fifth* and *Talley's Folly)* are highly realistic and beautifully detailed. The skeletal layout of the house in *Lemon Sky* recalls Willy Loman's impressionistic urban dwelling in Miller's *Salesman.* Sometimes a few architectural details establish the mise-en-scène on an otherwise bare stage (*Rill* and *Rimers*). The set for *Balm* is turned 180 degrees by the cast so that the audience has a quite different view of the action. The two married couples of *Louie* are equally at home in the same living room. The setting of a Wilson play is almost always a sensitive comment on the action.

Lanford Wilson has chronicled Americans at their best and worst over the last twenty-five years. By showing us what we were and what we are, it may be that he is showing us what we will become. His plays are a valid record of the life we have been living, for he is a literary mound builder, and when his work is excavated in some distant future in another century, people will know then what we were like in our time.

Appendix

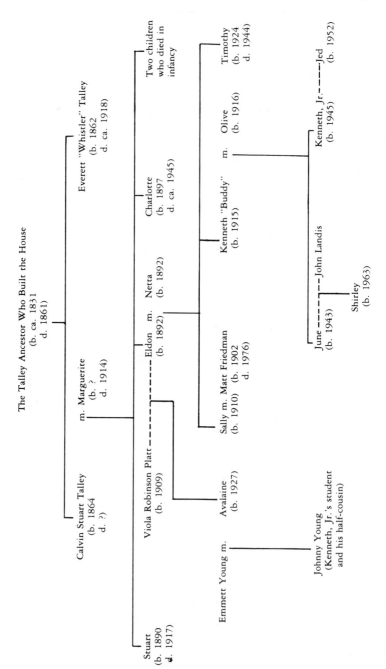

Talley Family Genealogy

Talley Family Chronology

ca. 1831　Birth of Talley ancestor, the father of Everett "Whistler" Talley and Calvin Stuart Talley; he "died at thirty. Built this house and didn't live a year in it."

1860　Talley farmhouse built.

1861　Death of Talley ancestor.

1862　Birth of Whistler Talley.

1864　Birth of Calvin Talley.

1890　Birth of Stuart Talley.

1892　Birth of Eldon Talley; Netta, his wife, is probably born this year.

1897　Birth of Charlotte (Aunt Lottie) Talley.

1902　Birth of Matt Friedman in Kaunas, Lithuania.

1910　Birth of Sally Talley; Harley Campbell is born the same year.

1911　Problems of Matt Friedman's family in Europe. Sometime before World War I, he makes his way, via South America, to the United States.

1911–1913　Approximate time setting of the projected play dealing with Whistler Talley.

1914　Calvin's wife, Marguerite, dies.

1915　Birth of Kenneth "Buddy" Talley.

1916　Birth of Olive Talley, Kenneth's wife.

1917　Death of Stuart Talley in World War I.

ca. 1918　Death of Whistler Talley.

1924　Birth of Timothy (Timmy) Talley.

ca. 1926　Sally Talley and Harley Campbell are high school sweethearts, eventually becoming engaged.

ca. 1927　Sally contracts tuberculosis and misses a year of high school. Her engagement to Harley Campbell is broken off.

ca. 1929   Harley Campbell attends Princeton University and has a romance with a girl from New Jersey whom he later marries.

1931   The factory owned by the Talley and Campbell families nearly goes broke. Harley Campbell's father commits suicide; Harley leaves school and works in the factory.

1941   Sally Talley takes a job at a hospital (O'Reilly General) in Springfield, Missouri.

1943   Matt Friedman vacations in the Lebanon, Missouri area and meets Sally Talley at a dance at the Shrine Mosque in Springfield.
Birth of June Talley.

1944   In February, Matt attempts to visit Sally at the hospital where she works in Springfield, but she refuses to see him.
In late June or early July, Timmy Talley is killed in the marines' assault on the Mariana Islands in the South Pacific.

1944   4 July: *Talley's Folly* and *Talley & Son.*

1945   Birth of Kenneth (Kenny) Talley, Jr.

1952   Birth of Jed Jenkins, Kenny Talley's lover.

ca. 1962–1967   Kenny, June, and John Landis, son of the local dentist, attend the University of California, Berkeley.

1971   Kenny retires from teaching.

1974   Jed begins to plant the garden on the grounds of the Talley farmhouse.

1976   Matt Friedman dies.

1976–1977   While Kenny spends the winter in Saint Louis, Jed cares for nurslings in the Talley house in Lebanon.

1977   In May, Kenny visits the high school in Lebanon where he is to teach in the autumn.

1977   4 July: act 1 of *Fifth of July;* 5 July: act 2 of *Fifth of July.* Sally attends Harley Campbell's funeral.

Notes and References

Preface

1. Albert Poland and Bruce Mailman, eds., *The Off Off Broadway Book* (Indianapolis, 1972), xvii.

Chapter One

1. Gene A. Barnett, Interview with Lanford Wilson, 17 December 1985.
2. Gene A. Barnett, "Recreating the Magic: An Interview with Lanford Wilson," *Ball State University Forum* 25 (1984):58.
3. Ibid., 57.
4. Mel Gussow, "Stage: Wilson's *Talley's Folly*," *New York Times*, 4 May 1979, sec. C, p. 3; Frank Rich, "Theater: Wilson's *Talley & Son*," *New York Times*, 23 October 1983, sec. C, p. 19; David Mamet, quoted in Mel Gussow, "Lanford Wilson on Broadway," *Horizon*, May 1980, 36.
5. Marguerite Feitlowitz, "An Interview with Lanford Wilson," *At the Rep* 1, no. 5 (1984).
6. Barnett, "Recreating the Magic," 57.
7. Barnett, Interview.
8. Barnett, "Recreating the Magic," 59.
9. Poland and Mailman, eds., *The Off Off Broadway Book*, xvii. For a tribute to Cino see Michael Smith, "Theatre Journal," *Village Voice*, 6 April 1967, 29.
10. Barnett, Interview.
11. Ibid.
12. Poland and Mailman, eds., *The Off Off Broadway Book*, 18.
13. Ann Dreher, "Lanford Wilson," in *Dictionary of Literary Biography* (Detroit, 1981), 7:358.

Chapter Two

1. *Home Free*, in *Balm in Gilead and Other Plays* (New York, 1965), 98. Further citations will be indicated in parentheses.
2. *The Bottle Harp*, unpublished manuscript. All quotations are from this manuscript.
3. William Hoffman, ed., *Gay Plays: The First Collection* (New York, 1979), xxiii.
4. Ibid., xxiv.

5. Ibid., xxvii.

6. Barnett, "Recreating the Magic," 71.

7. *The Madness of Lady Bright,* in *The Rimers of Eldritch* (New York, 1967), 88. Further citations will be indicated in parentheses.

8. *Ludlow Fair,* in *Balm in Gilead,* 82. Further citations will be indicated in parentheses.

Chapter Three

1. "Transitions," *New York Times,* 13 June 1984, sec. B, p. 2.

2. *Balm in Gilead,* in *Balm in Gilead,* 3. Further citations will be indicated in parentheses.

Chapter Four

1. *This Is the Rill Speaking,* in *The Rimers of Eldritch,* 102. Further citations will be indicated in parentheses.

2. *The Rimers of Eldritch,* in *The Rimers of Eldritch,* 3. Further citations will be indicated in parentheses.

Chapter Five

1. Barnett, "Recreating the Magic," 64.

2. *The Sand Castle,* in *The Sand Castle and Three Other Plays* (New York, 1970), 46. Further citations will be indicated in parentheses.

3. Barnett, Interview.

4. Ibid.

5. *Days Ahead,* in *The Rimers of Eldritch,* 65. Further citations will be indicated in parentheses.

6. *Wandering,* in *The Rimers of Eldritch,* 98. Further citations will be indicated in parentheses.

Chapter Six

1. John Corry, "Theater: *Gingham Dog* by Wilson Is Revived," *New York Times,* 1 February 1981, 46.

2. *The Gingham Dog* (New York, 1969), 44. Further citations will be indicated in parentheses.

Chapter Seven

1. Barnett, "Recreating the Magic," 60.

2. Frank Rich, "Theater: *Lemon Sky* by Lanford Wilson," *New York Times,* 12 December 1985, sec. C, p. 17.

3. Ross Wetzsteon, "The Most Populist Playwright," *New York,* 8 November 1982, 43.

4. *Lemon Sky* (New York, 1970), 33. Further citations will be indicated in parentheses.

5. Barnett, "Recreating the Magic," 59.

Chapter Eight

1. *Untitled Play,* unpublished manuscript. All quotations are from this manuscript.

2. Barnett, Interview.

3. Ibid.

4. *Sa Hurt?,* unpublished manuscript. All quotations are from this manuscript.

5. *Stoop,* in *The Sand Castle,* 67. Further citations will be indicated in parentheses.

6. Barnett, Interview.

7. *Victory on Mrs. Dandywine's Island,* in *The Great Nebula in Orion and Three Other Plays* (New York, 1973), 65. Further citations will be indicated in parentheses.

8. Barnett, Interview.

9. *Sextet (Yes),* in *The Sand Castle,* 73. Further citations will be indicated in parentheses.

10. *Ikke, Ikke, Nye, Nye, Nye,* in *The Great Nebula in Orion,* 55. Further citations will be indicated in parentheses.

11. Barnett, Interview.

12. Ibid.

13. Ibid.

14. *The Family Continues,* in *The Great Nebula in Orion,* 30. Further citations will be indicated in parentheses.

Chapter Nine

1. Scot Haller, "The Dramatic Rise of Lanford Wilson," *Saturday Review,* August 1981, 29.

2. John Simon, "Playing with Fire," *New York,* 13 February 1984, 68.

3. Barnett, "Recreating the Magic," 71.

4. *Serenading Louie,* rev. ed. (New York, 1984), 20. Further citations will be indicated in parentheses.

5. Benedict Nightingale, "For Lanford Wilson, Drama Begins at the Crossroads," *New York Times,* 12 February 1984, sec. 2, p. 5.

6. Barnett, "Recreating the Magic," 63.

Chapter Ten

1. Barnett, Interview.

2. *The Great Nebula in Orion,* in *The Great Nebula in Orion,* 19. Further citations will be indicated in parentheses.

3. *Brontosaurus* (New York, 1978), 8. Further citations will be indicated in parentheses.

4. *Bar Play,* unpublished manuscript. All quotations are from this manuscript.

Chapter Eleven

1. Barnett, "Recreating the Magic," 60–61.
2. Ibid, 61.
3. Ibid.
4. Haller, "The Dramatic Rise of Lanford Wilson," 28.
5. *The Hot-l Baltimore* (New York, 1973), 129. Further citations will be indicated in parentheses.
6. Patricia O'Haire, "That Seedy Old 'Hot l' Is Still Packin' 'Em In," *New York Daily News,* 30 November 1975, sec. 1, 16.
7. Ibid.
8. Guy Flatley, "Lanford Is One 'L' of a Playwright," *New York Times,* 22 April 1973, sec. 2, p. 21.
9. Ibid.
10. Ibid.
11. Ibid.

Chapter Twelve

1. Barnett, "Recreating the Magic," 62.
2. Mel Gussow, "Stage: *Mound Builders,*" *New York Times,* 4 February 1975, 35.
3. Allan Wallach, "Lanford Wilson," *Newsday,* 27 April 1980, 26.
4. Barnett, "Recreating the Magic," 71.
5. This chapter is based on the original edition.
6. *The Mound Builders* (New York, 1976), 4. Further citations will be indicated in parentheses.
7. Barnett, Interview.

Chapter Thirteen

1. Barnett, "Recreating the Magic," 70.
2. John J. O'Connor, "TV: 'Migrants,' a Drama That Portrays Poverty," *New York Times,* 1 February 1974, 61.
3. *The Migrants,* unpublished manuscript. All quotations are from this manuscript.
4. *Taxi,* unpublished manuscript. All quotations are from this manuscript.
5. Lee Hoiby, "Making Tennessee Williams Sing," *New York Times,* 13 June 1971, sec. 2, p. 17. The libretto is published by Belwin-Mills Publishing Corporation (New York, 1972).

6. Neal Ashby, "Five Views of *Summer and Smoke,*" *New York State Theater Magazine* 7, no. 23 (March 1972):11.

7. Mary Ann Feldman, "St. Paul's Summer," *Opera News,* 36 (September 1971):18.

Chapter Fourteen

1. *Fifth of July* (New York, 1979), 50. Further citations will be indicated in parentheses.

2. Letter to the author, 3 August 1981.

3. Barnett, Interview.

4. Wallach, "Lanford Wilson," 22.

5. Haller, "The Dramatic Rise of Lanford Wilson," 28.

6. William Raidy, "Lanford Eugene Wilson," Newark [N.J.] *Star Ledger,* 20 April 1980, sec. 4, p. 1.

7. Walter Kerr, "A Play in Which the Intrinsic Connections Are Missing," *New York Times,* 7 May 1978, sec. 2, p. 5; Richard Eder, "Theater: *5th of July* Is Staged," *New York Times,* 28 April 1978, sec. 3, p. 3. When the play moved to Broadway in 1980, the first word of the title was changed. *5th* became *Fifth,* and that is the spelling I have used throughout except when specifically citing the book (published as *5th of July*) or a review of the 1978 production.

8. Wallach, "Lanford Wilson," 26.

Chapter Fifteen

1. Mel Gussow, "Lanford Wilson on Broadway," *Horizon,* May 1980, 34.

2. Ibid.

3. Harold Clurman, "Theater," *Nation,* 15 March 1980, 316.

4. Mel Gussow, "Stage: Wilson's *Talley's Folly,*" *New York Times,* 4 May 1979, sec. C, p. 3; Walter Kerr, "Three New Plays, One 'A Treasure,' " *New York Times,* 13 May 1979, sec. 2, pp. 5, 24; Walter Kerr, "Stage: *Talley's Folly* by Lanford Wilson," *New York Times,* 21 February 1980, sec. C, p. 15.

5. Wallach, "Lanford Wilson," 32.

6. *Talley's Folly* (New York, 1981), 25. Further citations will be indicated in parentheses.

7. Letter to the author, 3 August 1981.

8. This scene is an *hommage* to Sam Shepard. See Barnett, "Recreating the Magic," 73.

9. Henry I. Schvey, "Images of the Past in the Plays of Lanford Wilson," *Essays on Contemporary American Drama,* ed. Hedwig Bock and Albert Wertheim (Munich, 1981), 237.

Chapter Sixteen

1. Ross Wetzsteon, "The Most Populist Playwright," 40; Clive Barnes, "Atoms and Angels: Six Characters in Search of the Meaning of Life," *New York Post,* 18 October 1982, 20; Brendan Gill, "The Theatre," *New Yorker,* 31 January 1983, 101; Barnes, "Atoms and Angels."

2. Walter Kerr, "Playwrights Are Growing Articulate Again," *New York Times,* 31 October 1982, sec. 2, p. 3; "Angels Fall," *Variety,* 27 October 1982, 84.

3. John Simon, "Too Much Heart? Too Much Brain?" *New York,* 1 November 1982, 81; and *New York,* 7 February 1983, 58.

4. *Angels Fall* (New York, 1983), 16. Further citations will be indicated in parentheses.

5. Barnett, "Recreating the Magic," 66.

6. Barnett, Interview.

Chapter Seventeen

1. *Thymus Vulgaris* (New York: 1982), 14. Further citations will be indicated in parentheses.

2. Lanford Wilson, "Trying to Discover Chekhov," in Playbill of the Hartford Stage Company, 20–22 March 1984, 5.

3. Ibid.

4. Mel Gussow, "Theater: Chekhov's *Three Sisters* in Hartford," *New York Times,* 6 April 1984, sec. C, p. 18.

5. *A Betrothal,* unpublished manuscript. Quotations are from this manuscript.

6. As he has often done, particularly in his Missouri plays, Wilson uses real place names. Ms. Joslyn is from Carmel, New York, approximately fifty miles northeast of New York City. Mr. Wasserman is from Mahopac, a few miles from Carmel. Castle Crampton and its gardens, to which the two characters refer in highly unflattering terms, is probably— and necessarily—a fictional name for the famous Caramoor at Katonah, New York.

Chapter Eighteen

1. John Simon, "Demirep," *New York,* 4 November 1985, 64.

2. *Talley & Son,* unpublished manuscript. All quotations are from this manuscript.

Chapter Nineteen

1. Michiko Kakutani, "I Write the World as I See It around Me," *New York Times,* 8 July 1984, sec. 2, p. 4.

Selected Bibliography

PRIMARY SOURCES

1. Published Works
Angels Fall. New York: Hill & Wang, 1983.
Balm in Gilead and Other Plays. 1965. Reprint New York: Hill & Wang, 1965.
Brontosaurus. New York: Dramatists Play Service, 1978.
5th of July. New York: Hill & Wang, 1979.
The Gingham Dog. New York: Dramatists Play Service, 1969.
The Great Nebula in Orion and Three Other Plays. New York: Dramatists Play Service, 1973.
The Hot-l Baltimore. New York: Hill & Wang, 1973.
Lemon Sky. New York: Dramatists Play Service, 1970.
The Mound Builders. New York: Hill & Wang, 1976.
The Rimers of Eldritch and Other Plays. New York: Hill & Wang, 1967.
The Sand Castle and Three Other Plays. New York: Dramatists Play Service, 1970.
Serenading Louie, rev. ed. New York: Dramatists Play Service, 1984.
Summer and Smoke. Libretto for an opera by Lee Hoiby from a play by Tennessee Williams. New York: Belwin-Mills Corporation, 1972.
Talley's Folly. New York: Hill & Wang, 1981.
Three Sisters, by Anton Chekhov. Translated by Lanford Wilson. New York: Dramatists Play Service, 1984.
Thymus Vulgaris. New York: Dramatists Play Service, 1982.

2. Unpublished Materials (in possession of the author)
Bar Play
A Betrothal
The Bottle Harp
Burn This
The Migrants
Sa Hurt?
A Tale Told
Talley & Son
Taxi
Untitled Play

SECONDARY SOURCES

Albright, William. "Lanford Wilson, From 'Burn' to 'Balm.' " *Houston Post,* 2 February 1986, sec. F, p. 3. A recent interview on *Balm, Burn This,* the Talley plays, and a possible sixth play on Shirley Talley.

Baker, Rob. "Lanford Wilson's Family Affair." *New York Daily News,* 5 June 1981, sec. M, pp. 2–3. Discusses *A Tale Told,* methods of composition, the play as autobiography, a play on Whistler Talley, and the playwright's family background.

Barnett, Gene A. "Recreating the Magic: An Interview with Lanford Wilson." *Ball State University Forum.* 25 (Spring 1984):57–74. Deals with Wilson's early interest in the theater, influences, themes, development of plays, writing for television, and writing for the Circle Rep.

Berkvist, Robert. "Lanford Wilson—Can He Score on Broadway?" *New York Times,* 17 February 1980, sec. 2, pp. 1, 33. On the playwright's background, early plays, themes, the Missouri years, writing a thriller, and royalties.

Blau, Eleanor. "How Lanford Wilson Writes with Actors in Mind." *New York Times,* 27 January 1983, sec. 3, p. 15. Wilson describes how he tailors roles for certain actors, sometimes to use qualities he sees in them, sometimes as a challenge to them.

Dasgupta, Gautam. "Lanford Wilson." In *American Playwrights, A Critical Survey,* edited by Bonnie Marranca and Gautam Dasgupta, 27–39. New York: Drama Books Specialists, 1981. On Wilson as a playwright of "poeticized reality," whose principal theme is the passing of time; his techniques; a brief survey of major and some minor plays down through *Talley's Folly; Hot-l, Rimers,* and *Talley's Folly* "skillfully integrate the characters' private ambitions and desires within the universe they belong in."

Dreher, Ann. "Lanford Wilson." In *Dictionary of Literary Biography,* 7:350–68. Detroit: Gale, 1981. A long biographical entry that deals briefly but effectively with all the playwright's work up through *Talley's Folly.*

Flatley, Guy. "Lanford Is One 'L' of a Playwright." *New York Times,* 22 April 1973, sec. 2, pp. 1, 21. The playwright comments on *Lady Bright* and the characters of *Hot-l Baltimore.*

Freedman, Samuel G. "Lanford Wilson Enjoys a Triumph over Time." *New York Times,* 26 December 1985, sec. 3, p. 13. On the late 1985 revival of *Lemon Sky;* the playwright is concerned whether or not the early plays will hold up in revival.

Gussow, Mel. "Lanford Wilson on Broadway." *Horizon,* May 1980, 30–
37. Biographical background and career up through *Talley's Folly;*
Wilson is "as old fashioned as Chekhov"; his art is "a quest for
durability, for attachment"; "begins as a regionalist but becomes
national."

Haller, Scot. "The Dramatic Rise of Lanford Wilson." *Saturday Review,*
August 1981, 26–29. The playwright's Missouri background, years
in Chicago, early days in New York City, the Talley plays, *Fifth of
July, Louie,* and other works.

Hoffman, William M. Introduction to *Gay Plays: The First Collection.* New
York: Avon Books, 1979. The "gay play" defined; "gay play" versus
"gay theater"; a brief history of the treatment of homosexuality in
the theater, particularly on Broadway and Off-Broadway since 1950.

Kakutani, Michiko. " 'I Write the World as I See It around Me.' " *New
York Times,* 8 July 1984, sec. 2, pp. 4, 6. The creation of *Balm;* for
Wilson, "speech patterns form the basis of a character, and characters
form the basis of a play"; creating roles for actors; plays as "sermons";
his Missouri past.

Kellman, Barnet. "The American Playwright in the Seventies: Some Problems & Perspectives." *Theater Quarterly* 8 (1978):43–58. Wilson on
a panel with six other playwrights. He speaks of the role of the agent,
commissions, workshop productions versus Broadway; the writer's
involvement in a production; Hill and Wang; the television series
based on *Hot-l.*

O'Haire, Patricia. "That Seedy Old 'Hot l' Is Still Packin' 'Em In." *New
York Daily News,* 30 November 1975, sec. L, p. 16. On the development of *Hot-l,* which began as a trilogy; the hotel setting; Baltimore
as a rail center.

Paul, John Steven. "Who Are You? Who Are We?" *Cresset* 43 (September
1980):25–27. In asking the question "Who are you?" of Matt and
Sally, Wilson places *Talley's Folly* in the mainstream of American
drama, which is "a drama of character."

Poland, Albert, and Bruce Mailman, eds. *The Off Off Broadway Book.*
Indianapolis: Bobbs-Merrill, 1972. A very useful record of the founding and early days of Off-Off-Broadway, brief histories of the Caffe
Cino and La Mama, the plays presented there, and their dates up to
1972.

Schvey, Henry I. "Images of the Past in the Plays of Lanford Wilson."
In *Essays on Contemporary American Drama,* edited by Hedwig Bock
and Albert Wertheim, 225–40. Munich: Max Huber Verlag, 1981.
An in-depth commentary on the uses of the past in *Hot-l, Mound
Builders,* and *Talley's Folly.*

Smith, Michael. Introduction to *Eight Plays from Off-Off Broadway,* edited

PR
37
E88
981

by Nick Orzel and Michael Smith, 1–16. Indianapolis: Bobbs-Merrill, 1966. A brief history of the Off-Off-Broadway movement by one who was closely involved in it.

Soric, Peggy. "Sound Catcher." [Springfield, Missouri] *News-Leader,* 30 January 1983, sec. G, p. 1. An interview shortly after the opening of *Angels Fall;* discusses Wilson's ability to capture the rhythms of speech; the sounds of his characters are "always at the heart of what I was trying to do"; remarks on the use of the Missouri background and his youth there.

Swift, Elliott. "The Life and Times of Playwright Lanford Wilson." *Hamptons,* 11 August 1983, 12–13, 16. An interview dealing with the formation of the Circle Rep, the writing of *Lady Bright* and *Hot-l,* English plays on Broadway, and advice to young playwrights.

Wallach, Allan. "Lanford Wilson." *Newsday,* 27 April 1980, 21–22, 26, 32–33. A good interview focusing on the Talley plays, the Chicago period, *Fifth of July, Mound Builders,* and *Talley's Folly.*

Wetzsteon, Ross. "The Most Populist Playwright." *New York,* 8 November 1982, 40, 43–45. Focuses on *Angels Fall,* the first months in New York City, the meeting with Marshall Mason, the background of *Lemon Sky,* and the formation of Circle Rep.

Wilson, Lanford. "Observations of a Resident Playwright." *New York Times,* 23 April 1978, sec. 2, p. 5. Wilson's comments about working with and writing for the members of the Circle Repertory Company.

Winter, Helmut. "Lanford Wilson: *The Rimers of Eldritch.*" In *Das amerikanische Drama der Gegenwart,* edited by Herbert Grabes, 120–32. Kronberg: Athenäum Verblg, 1976. *Rimers* is a reversal of the American ideal of the simple life of the average person in social harmony. The radical tone of Wilson's condemnation of small-town narrow-mindedness puts it in the developmental line that began with *Winesburg, Ohio* and *Main Street.*

Witham, Barry B. "Images of America: Wilson, Weller and Horovitz." *Theatre Journal* 34 (May 1982):223–32. Wilson uses Independence Day "to analyze a specific dramatic conflict as well as to assess the American temperament in the mid 1970s." *Fifth of July* is about "a return to the past in order to confront the future." The play abounds with images of growth that "underscore the need for change."

Wynne, Peter. "Wilson Blooms on Broadway." *Sunday* [Bergen County, New Jersey] *Record,* 16 November 1980, sec. F, p. 13–14. The playwright and horticulture, the characters in *Fifth of July,* the Talley cycle.

Index

DATE DUE

JUN 9 '89			
MAY 27 '89 S			
AUG 25 '89			
DEC 14 '89 S			
Dec 26 '89			
JUN 4 '91 S			
GAYLORD			PRINTED IN U S A